Life:

I Do Believe In Spirit

Life's magical, enjoyable journey.

by

Kenneth Routson

Fairfield, Ohio

Copyright © 1998 by Kenneth Routson
All rights reserved. Printed in the U.S.A.

No part of this publication may be reproduced or transmitted in any form by any means, electronic or mechanical, including photocopy, recording, or any other information storage and retrieval system or by any other system now known or to be invented, without permission in writing from the publisher; except for the quotation of brief passages for review and/or publicity purposed for inclusion in a magazine, newspaper, broadcast, or related media.

The author and those associated with this book do not dispense medical advice nor prescribe the use of any technique discussed in this book as a form of treatment for physical, medical or emotional problems without the advice of a physician. The intent of this book is to offer information. In the event you use any of the information in this book for yourself, which is your constitutional right, the author and those associated with this book assume no responsibility for your actions.

Quoted portions or material otherwise attributed appears with permission or relates to matters of communication within the public domain. Every effort has been made to secure prior authorization, and any non-compliance is purely inadvertent. Grateful acknowledgment is made for all such instances including Carin Waddell/*Haré* and Gorden Stonehouse/*Amel* and Jeff King/*Teach*.

Publisher's Cataloging-in-Publication
(Provided by Quality Books, Inc.)

Routson, Kenneth.
    Internal life : I do believe in spirit / by Ken Routson. -- 1st ed.
    p. cm.
    LCCN: 98-61171
    ISBN: 1-891067-02-8

    1. Self-help techniques. 2. Self-realization.
3. Success. 4. Spirit writings. I. Title.

BF637.S4R68 1998   158.1
                      QB198-1576

Cover Design by: Nikki Clark
Layout and Design by: Denise J. Lasley
Printed by: Bookmasters, Inc.
Published by: Tulip Press, P.O. Box 181212, Fairfield, OH 45018

First Edition   10 9 8 7 6 5 4 3 2 1

TABLE OF CONTENTS ❖ ❖ ❖ ❖ ❖ ❖ ❖

	PREFACE	i
	INTRODUCTION	iv
1	Creating My Life	1
2	Spiritual Journey: Implementing the Material	15
3	Looking Back: Releasing My Dungeon Children	19
4	Intro-Spection	33
5	New Realities: Do I Believe in Ghosts?	43
6	Meeting *Amel:* I do Believe in Spirits	51
7	Communicating With the Spirit World	71
8	Time For A Change	81
9	Coming Home	95
10	*Teach:* Exploring My Beliefs/Consciousness	103
11	Internal Life	169
12	Fictional Short Story: Or Is It?	179
	APPENDIX: Questions & Answers	i

ACKNOWLEDGMENTS ❖ ❖ ❖ ❖ ❖ ❖ ❖

Many thanks go to Gordon Stonehouse for giving me permission to use material from *Amel*, and to Jeff King for his consent to use some of my correspondence with *Teach*.

My special thanks go to Denise Lasley (editor for Tulip Press), Merrianne Johnson, Michelle Moderbacher and Del Lasley for their assistance and friendship.

Finally, my appreciation to Leslie Stewart and to my parents, teachers (seen and unseen), brothers, sisters and other relatives, and to all my many friends and students for their love and support.

DEDICATION ❖ ❖ ❖ ❖ ❖ ❖ ❖

I dedicate this book to all conscious-life creators, and to George and Mary Coleman (no longer on this side of life) who were like grandparents to me, and to the Townsend Family, the Ward Family and the Williams Family, who all treated *me* like family.

This book is also dedicated to the following individuals who, despite opposition, acted upon the inner guidance that provided them with the inspiration and courage to make a difference:

Jane Roberts
Aurore Dudevant (George Sand)
Herman Hesse
Mahatma Ghandi
Ralph Emerson
Albert Einstein
Carl Jung
Benjamin Franklin
Thomas Jefferson
Martin Luther King
Bob Dylan
The Beatles
J. Krishnamurti

Peter, Paul and Mary
Joan Baez
Jimmy Carter
Victoria Woodhull
Phil Donahue
Robert Butts
Nelson Mandella
Henry Thoreau
Helen Keller
Oprah Winfrey
Edgar Cayce
Kahlil Gibran

PREFACE ❖ ❖ ❖ ❖ ❖ ❖ ❖

I would like to invite you to join me and embark upon an exciting adventure, a journey inward to a new frontier — **Internal Life**. This quest is about self-exploration, self-acceptance and self-love, as we explore how each one of *our* selves is connected to each *other* self and how essentially we are all of *one cosmic divine* self.

We live in a time when many people believe that unpleasant circumstances just happen to people and that we have no control over external events. We have a collective culture that believes that victimhood is socially acceptable behavior; a senseless world where fate, luck and accidents rule. Society needs pioneers to introduce the masses to the metaphysical universal law: *We all create our own reality through our intentions, beliefs, expectations and emotions.* Everyone we meet and everything we do, including all relationships, events and experiences in our outer world, are all merely a reflection of our inner world.

Throughout history, humans have searched the external frontiers: first man explored undeveloped land upon the earth, then the ocean and now outer space. The pursuit to heal sickness has also been directed toward finding external causes and cures. Until now we have been more or less ego driven, searching for our true self and for God outside ourselves. We have been obsessive-compulsive in attempting to find someone or something to make us whole. Somewhere along the way humans have disconnected themselves from their source — *God* — and from the rest of earth's creaturehood — *nature*. Consequently, humankind has contaminated its consciousness with hate, fear, uncertainty, doubt, greed and basic powerlessness.

For self-serving reasons, man has defined God in his image instead of examining and intuitively feeling what God really *is*. Because we have a limited image of God as a patriarchal figure, we have created self-imposed boundaries of beliefs and behaviors that limit our growth and potential by creating an artificial veil separating our inner, or *spiritual*, reality from our outer *physical* reality. Once we can break through this veil, we can integrate our combined male, female inner/spiritual self with our outer/physical self and live up to our full potential. Only then will we be able to actualize the power and abilities of a human being, realizing that the only limitations we have are those that our ego accepts. Although there is much criticism of the ego, the ego is necessary in physical reality because it assists the personality maneuver in space and time. However, in our society we let our ego dominate while we repress, depress and suppress other aspects of self such as intuition, sensitivity and awareness. When we can understand the necessary functions of the ego, we can achieve a natural, healthy balance allowing other portions of our inner-self to collaborate and work cooperatively in concert with the ego. As we become more inner-directed we will see outer changes in the way we live including our technology, business, education and culture in general which will bring us to new frontiers from cyberspace to inner-space. Through conscious dreaming or by going into a trance we will be able to enter the cosmic inner-net where we can explore *past* historical realities or *future* earth, as well as other physical and non-physical realities!

This spiritual awakening will evolve with the psychic expansion of self and the embracing of the spirit world that the ego-self has so long been frightened to consider. It is my intent in this book to encourage those of you who have been reluctant to explore your internal life to acknowledge your inner-self, angels and spirit teachers and to learn the importance of, and how to consciously connect to them. It is my objective that by sharing my life's challenges and stories of how I overcame my erroneous beliefs and became aware of the many *co-incidences* that turned into meaningful opportunities for me, that others may learn how to consciously create *their* life of choice.

The common theme that seems to run through all inspirational teachings is the power of love and acceptance.

Love is the most important and the most potent natural universal source!

Unconditional love effects every atom, molecule, chemical and the psyche of biological matter. Love radiates electromagnetically throughout the known and unknown universes. So you would think that self-acceptance would be a simple thing to accomplish. But for me it has been a long process. Many people mistake self-love and acceptance with selfishness. Selfishness is when we meet our needs at the expense of others. Selfishness usually involves control and manipulation. Only when we can love, accept and express ourselves can we truly love anyone else. *"Love your neighbor as you love yourself."* When we unite our selves with our inner-knowing and power while loving and accepting ourselves, then and only then can we transform disease into health, poverty into abundance, unhappiness into joy. Each person will be vibrant, fulfilled and will feel whole and they will contribute positively to the whole of nature by just being themselves.

Before reading any further, I suggest that each of you start a personal journal to write your own stories and note any ideas or feelings that may surface as you read this book. Start writing about your childhood and adulthood and the many *co-incidences* that actually proved to be stepping stones to greater opportunities. In addition, use your journal to enter your dreams (both evening and day dreams) so you too can explore your **INTERNAL LIFE!**

INTRODUCTION ❖ ❖ ❖ ❖ ❖ ❖ ❖

It is my intention to inspire my readers to recognize the seemingly accidental *co-incidences* and serendipitous experiences in your own life, and how to use those clues and follow your internal guidance to make synchronicities happen. Everyone — and everything — has its own *internal life*. You create your reality from the inside out by being inner-directed. You can only do this by acting on your instincts or *little voice*. Synchronicity is about being in the right place at the right time. By the time you finish this book, you will be consciously looking for synchronicity in your day-to-day living, as you realize that this can be the road to fulfilling opportunities and a way to consciously create your reality of choice.

There are no accidents or coincidences. Those events you previously rationalized as coincidental are synchronicities designed to create a fulfilling event or experience. Have you ever had an intense inner (gut) feeling, or a sudden intuitive insight, or perhaps a *knowing*? As you read about my spiritual evolution, you may recall the instances in your life when you didn't listen to your inner urges and made decisions based on outer circumstance, such as fear or previous conditioning, that resulted in a less than favorable life experience. Or you may remember a fantastic and/or beneficial event that seemed to miraculously and spontaneously present itself. I, like many others, believe our purpose for living is to learn how our thoughts, beliefs, feelings and visions create our reality. Your external life is the reflection, outpicturing and extension of your *internal life*. Take 100% personal responsibility and you will consciously create the ideal life of your choice.

You as an individual, and *we* as a collective consciousness, in internal partnership with the *earth/universal consciousness* are in labor. The new birth will bring a more conscious, aware, enlightened civilization that accepts the idea that one co-creates his/her reality, and will indeed consciously create a world of love, joy, abundance and fulfillment.

In the coming years, every human being will be inwardly greeted and inspired with new epiphanies in tandem with unusual outer experiences of change and challenge. Your feelings about every area of life will be changing as you shed your old beliefs and transform into a new, powerful, fulfilled and loving self. If you examine history, you will see a reoccurring theme: a quest for freedom. The entire world culture will reclaim its power and will finally have that freedom sought after by many civilizations.

Collectively we are experiencing the macrovision of that rebirth with an insatiable urge to be at peace with self and to allow our *real* inner-self to emerge into the new, manifested state. The final chapter in the continuing earth saga of humans in search of freedom will come when we realize that we have created our own bondage and we have unconsciously chosen to hide the keys that can provide us with our freedom. It is now time to reclaim your power and use the key of *natural awareness* to unlock the eternal resources of your inner-God selves.

It is an awareness that there is no one greater or lesser than yourself. It is the knowingness that each person is God. When you realize that you are not separate from God, then you can begin to move away from man-made rules, regulations and the limitations they breed. With these epiphanies, you will *know* that we are all equal. Because of *freewill*, there is no mandate or directive from God, your higher self, or anyone else to force you to be powerful, fulfilled, joyful and enlightened. But you create your reality — your strengths as well as your *believed* weaknesses — and you have the same, equal opportunities as everybody else.

Journey to the last frontier to be explored — *inner freedom.* May this book help you recognize your own fears and doubts and learn to release them so you can embrace your *Godhood* while discovering that this freedom and power has always been available to you *internally*. May this book help you turn your synchronicities into magical experiences as you come to understand that everything in your world is a reflection of your *internal life.*

Kenneth Routson
October, 1998

Chapter 1
Creating My Life

How often have you asked yourself — or perhaps asked others — about birth, life, death, eternity, infinity or whether or not life exists elsewhere in the universe?

I remember as a child sitting on the porch with my mother, gazing into the summer sky and asking her, *"If a rocket would go straight up, how far would it go?"* Mom's response was, *"To heaven."* And even though I couldn't express my curiosity verbally, I remember thinking, *"Then what's on the other side of heaven?"*

My mother had a complicated pregnancy with me, and as a result I was born with learning disabilities that limited my ability to communicate until I was in the 7th grade. Initially, speech therapists and teachers thought I was developmentally disabled (mentally retarded). They referred my parents to a psychologist, who eventually relieved their fears when his testing determined that my intelligence quotient was quite normal. Even as my verbal skills grew, I still felt ill at ease expressing myself to others. I believe I chose my parents and either created or acquiesced to all the events in my life, including the inability to express myself as well as my difficulty relating to people. I think this afforded me the opportunity to explore the inner realities that consequently led me to the realization that we do indeed create our own personal reality and co-create all the other events in our lives.

If only I had trusted my little voice from the very beginning . . . I would have eliminated much suffering. But it wasn't until later in my life that I could embrace with confidence the idea that my internal impulses were the valid, authentic and real perception of my life as opposed to the messages that came from my outer every day life from man-made authorities like religion, science, medicine and education. These perceptions were, for the most part, extremely limiting and often erroneous.

Recently there have been many books written about metaphysics, ghosts, entities, reincarnation, cosmic consciousness, psychic phenomena and quantum physics. Even religion is showing signs of significant transformation, especially when you hear fundamentalists echoing clichés like, *"Our church is different, we are spiritual, not religious."* Meanwhile corporations and organizations are reorganizing, using the concept of the 90's: *the new paradigm..*

Throughout this book I will explore the nature of consciousness and internal realities and how they create our outer world. And I will discuss the evolution now taking place on our planet and how significant transformations are taking place in every area of our lives. These transformations will come about as more and more individuals wake to the realization that there are no victims and that we are all divine, with the awesome power to create a joyful, healthy, prosperous reality. As you become more aware, you will realize that you only need to protect yourself from your *own* fears, doubts and guilt because everything in your daily life is an out-picturing of your *internal* life.

I was a medical aid supervisor for a high school program for students with severe physical disabilities. Before the advent of inclusion (mainstreaming students with disabilities), these pupils were in segregated programs and usually graduated after grammar school. Our program for high school individuals, developed in 1972, was one of the first in the country. Although I didn't have a college degree, I developed much of the curriculum along with other teachers, including Shirley Turner, Kathy Winter and Beth Ferris. Since we were pioneers in this field, and because the national and state boards of education were not imposing many rigid requirements such as grades, required class time or tests, we were free to create a program we felt was appropriate to meet the needs of these students. I feel my most significant input was selling the teachers on establishing a free school that encouraged functional learning in a happy environment — an environment that enhanced self esteem, self direction, creativity and skill development to assist people with disabilities to become independent, happy individuals. Years later most of the special education programs that have been developed use the theories of functional learning, and fortunately, many of them still stress self-esteem.

One of the greatest contributions Beth and Kathy provided was introducing the class members to many different people and learning experiences. Each month they would invite a chef to cook a foreign dish or a variety of speakers to discourse on diverse subjects. The speaker I remember best was a psychic named Maggie Price who spoke to the class on psychic phenomena and concluded her message with brief psychic readings. Several times she returned her gaze to me and revealed a specific prophecy. My response was extremely rude; I literally laughed in her face. I remember her following comments most vividly. *"You, with the beard and overalls, I see you in an old cemetery. There is one cemetery you go to often and this vision also symbolizes to me that you will be communicating with the dead. You may laugh now, but I think you will become a spiritual leader."*

Really, this was too much! Me, a spiritual leader! At that point in my life I certainly didn't consider myself a spiritual *person,* let alone a spiritual *leader.* During this time I acknowledged myself to be an agnostic and although I did go through a brief spiritual period earlier (and I talk about that in another chapter), I always felt that once you were dead that's it! I took comfort from identifying with another staff member named T.J., who was an avowed atheist. We shared similar philosophies about government policies too, especially about Vietnam,

Little did I know on that day that the joke was on me. My current ego would not accept such nonsense, even though I profess I *did* believe in the power of the mind and rational thoughts.

Over the next few years, I met a lot of new people and things began to happen that caused me to reflect on Maggie Price's prediction. In early 1973, I moved out of my parent's home into my first apartment. My roommate, Bruce Fanelli, was the most androgynous male I had ever met. This was a new experience for me. The friends I grew up with were conditioned that men should be masculine and women should be feminine. Perhaps this was one of the many reasons I felt that the stork had dropped me on the wrong planet. In retrospect, I've always felt more feminine than masculine, but in my earlier days I suppressed those feminine characteristics in order to survive.

Bruce was an extremely gentle and sensitive soul. However, he was physically strong, and he loved nature and would frequently go off on primitive camping trips. Bruce reminded me of my image of what the man Jesus may have been like. In those early years, many people just assumed Bruce and I were gay. When I look back on my life, I can see how I attracted and chose various kinds of people, cultures and experiences during my growing up years to prepare and create my future. I have always felt a deep affinity for Bruce that would continue throughout my life. Later in this book I will take you back to my childhood days to illustrate how we choose and attract various kinds of people, cultures, and experiences in our growing up years to prepare and create our future.

Nineteen seventy-four was an extremely important year — it was a crossroad, a new chapter in my life, providing the catalysts that introduced me to more people and events that would transform my life. I had moved to a new world — the world of suburbia. After much reluctance and apprehension, I made friends with, and subsequently became more or less accepted as a member of a family in a well-to-do neighborhood south of Dayton. The Holders were from North Carolina, which in itself was a hurdle for me to overcome. As a *Northerner* all my life, I grew up suspicious of the gracious ways of *Southerners*. My prejudice was also fanned by a left-over belief from the '60's that "*money is the root of all evil*" and I was extremely suspicious of businessmen. Max Holder was a successful executive married to Jane, a fascinating person who would be very instrumental in helping me view the world in a different light. Jane had polio when she was nine which left her a paraplegic. I was amazed at Jane's accomplishments: she grew up in a wheel chair, graduated from college, taught school, gave birth and raised a son. Their son, Walker, would become like a brother to me.

The Holders introduced me to many people in their social circle. I had the opportunity to see that many affluent people were generous enough to provide opportunities as well as resources for those less fortunate. This was exemplified through the years as I saw the things the Holders did for their present community and heard stories of how involved they had been back home in North Carolina in projects such as a prison mentor program.

Jane's entrance into my life was timely because in February of 1974 my father lost his leg from diabetes and she helped him see that life in a wheelchair didn't have to be limiting. This brought about a new beginning for me and my relationship with my father that would lead me to experience unconditional love.

About that time, Jane introduced me to a psychic she had met through a doctor who practiced holistic medicine. This person also conducted dream workshops based on Edgar Casey work with dream interpretations. Yes, I was skeptical about reincarnation and definitely didn't think I wanted to be communicating with spooks, but I've always had a profound interest in dreams and the power of the mind. I attended several of these dream classes and although they were interesting I had a problem with interpreting a dream based on the theory that symbols mean certain things. Intuitively I felt that dreams were significant but only an individual could interpret their own symbols according to what each symbol represented to them

Creating My Life 7

personally. A rose to one person may symbolize springtime but for someone else it may represent a funeral. And besides, depending on the period in one's life, a dream of death could signify the end of a relationship or a job and the advent of something new as opposed to the more obvious interpretation that someone will die. Now I don't know if Edgar Casey believed in an absolute set of dream symbols, but I decided to start my own dream study group where individuals could explore their own dreams and develop their own symbols and meanings, sharing them with the group.

During the mid-seventies, Jane Holder was going through a process called *Rolfing* and introduced me to the Rolfer (practitioner), Dale Townsend. *Rolfing*, technically referred to as Structural Integration, consists of a series of messages, the purpose of which is to realign the body to it's natural balance, simultaneously eliminating the rigidity and tightness in muscles that are stressed from emotional and physical wear and tear. By this time I had read many self-help books including the popular *ERRONEOUS ZONES* written by Wayne Dyer, and I yearned for the opportunity to actually meet a person who had eliminated all of their erroneous zones. Finally I felt I had met such a person. Dale was a handsome, tanned energetic, enthusiastic young man with an apparently strong physique. *Rolfing* cost $40.00 a session and many of Jane's wealthy friends thought that was expensive but although I only made $3,000 a year at that point in my life I had an insatiable urge to learn more about this technique. Dale informed me of a workshop he was conducting on the topic of "Changing Negative Mental Patterns to Positive Affirmatives". I attended the workshop and although I was skeptical, I was nevertheless very intrigued. In particular, the following concepts that were discussed did provoke a lot of thought and I left the seminar with a curiosity to learn more:

- *There are no accidents.*
- *Anyone attending the workshop could become a millionaire.*
- *Most illnesses are self-created.*
- *You can change your life through the utilization of affirmations and visualizations.*

After class that Saturday evening I stopped in at one of my favorite places, *The Shed*, a bar that was frequented by University of Dayton students. As I sat at the bar drinking a beer, the barmaid, who had never spoken to me before, said, *"You have a beautiful aura."*

I was astounded. I responded with, *"You're not into that eastern religion crap are you?"*

She didn't answer me. But when she brought me another beer, I tried again. I told her that I believed in the power of the mind and that I definitely believed that your future could be predicted in your dreams. *"However,"* I said, *" I do not believe in reincarnation, meditation or auras and I enjoy meat too much to ever become a vegetarian."*

She replied, *"I believe you create your life through your beliefs and what you think."*

I was astonished. *"This is too much. You sound just like the leader of the workshop I went to today. Yes, I believe in the power of the mind, but not to the extent I heard discussed today."* She explained that she was once dubious herself, but after reading a series of books on the subject she was now convinced. However, I was not.

The next morning I went to visit my dad, maintaining a routine I had established several months earlier after he lost his leg to complications from his diabetes and was forced to retire from his job at the post office. My mom, who worked at the time for Miami Valley Hospital in Dayton, is a devout Christian — a practicing Lutheran — but she also had an interest in the supernatural and esoteric philosophy. It wasn't unusual to find various books at home on these subjects. My father thought the entire subject matter, including astrology, was absurd and he often expressed his opinion that my mom should, in his words, *"Stay away from such garbage."*

As my father and I watched the Cincinnati Reds game on television he began to doze off for an afternoon nap. Suddenly a book in a bookcase across the room drew my attention as if it was a very powerful magnet pulling me towards it. I picked it up and as I skimmed through the pages I got the sense that the basic theme of the book was all about how *you create your reality.* It was the author's general agnosticism and intense skepticism that pulled me into the book, because it made me feel that this person evidently was not gullible or following a dogma blindly. The book was titled the *SETH MATERIAL,* and little did I know at the time that this incident would be the first step to discovering my life's purpose.

That same Sunday evening I returned to my favorite bar to share yet another *co-incidence* with the barmaid. After some more conversation, I discovered that the readings she had referred to the night before included the book that practically jumped out at me from the bookcase at my parents' house. First thing Monday morning I purchased several *Seth* books. I began to spend more and more time at my apartment or sitting quietly in the woods reading the *SETH MATERIAL,* but I found myself periodically falling asleep. Years later when I began to conduct workshops throughout the country, I discovered that other people reading the *SETH MATERIAL* often had a similar experience. It definitely wasn't because of boredom. The best I can conclude is that this sleep state allows other levels of knowing, especially one's inner-self, to help process the Seth information.

Nevertheless, discovering *Seth* was like finding an old, lost friend! It was fascinating. As I read the author's introduction of the *SETH MATERIAL*, I was delighted to find someone else who as a child had difficulty accepting the *traditional* Father-God and questioned that if there was in fact a chauvinistic deity, he must be very insecure. Like myself, the author, Jane Roberts, grew up wondering how any intelligent person could buy into believing in a supreme being who demands to be worshipped and feared and who commands unquestioning obedience. As I read further, my own recollections of childhood conflict began to surface. I remembered asking my Sunday school teacher, *"Is it true that all the blacks kids in Africa will go to hell if they are not baptized even if they never hear about Jesus or the bible?"* Of course, the reply was, *"Yes, according to the bible."* How many religions still preach this absurdity? I was raised Lutheran and during my confirmation classes you can imagine the debates I had with the minister.

Jane Roberts was raised Catholic, and although she seemed to have a healthy skepticism she didn't appear to be as angry or bitter as I was about church, God, and patriarchal and hierarchical chauvinistic dogma. I have since forgiven myself for the agony and conflict I subjected myself to, and realize the people who subscribe to those archaic, guilt ridden religious beliefs are simply doing the best they can. Yes, I've let go of the anger, but it continues to surprise me that so many intelligent people still believe in such man-made nonsense and I wonder how many sheep in the church pews have even listened — let alone questioned

— the scriptures or the words to the hymns they sing. I can understand why people go to church for the fellowship and social aspects organized religion provides. Actually, I still enjoy going to church periodically to enjoy the organ music and some of the rituals that touch my emotional chords and provide me with some fulfillment.

As I read more about Jane Roberts, and her artist husband, Rob, I learned we share some fundamental beliefs including a similar skepticism and reluctance to believe in the possibility of reincarnation. At the time I began delving into the *SETH MATERIAL*, I was conducting a dream study group where the concept of reincarnation came up from time to time and I often referred to Jane's material to back up my initial skepticism.

My fascination and curiosity about psychic phenomenon, as well as the power of the mind, have always been intense. Coincidentally, as I continued to flip through the pages of the *SETH MATERIAL,* I discovered that Jane and I also share this common interest. Jane had written a book entitled *HOW TO DEVELOP YOUR ESP POWER* and she also held weekly ESP classes. In this book, Jane discussed her first psychic experience which occurred on September 9, 1963. She had settled down to write some poetry, as she was often accustomed to doing, when she suddenly found herself connected to an energizing, intensive and pulsating ideating energy. This intuitive energy imparted inspirational ideas. The information came so fast, and the ideas flowed so smoothly, that before she knew it Jane had a completed manuscript she titled *THE PHYSICAL UNIVERSE AS IDEA CONSTRUCTION.* Jane later wrote how even though she was initially skeptical, she felt a sense of knowing and discerned this information flow as more of a feeling then a mental manifestation even though it had a profound intellectual slant. This experience led Jane to several epiphanies: *We form physical matter; everything has its own consciousness; all physical objects are projected ideas; and we are individual expressions of energy materialized within physical bodies.*

Soon after this initial experience, Jane and Rob began to experiment with a Ouija board and to their surprise and amazement they began receiving information from *Seth*. Approximately a week later, on December 15, 1963, Seth began to speak through Jane. I was amazed at the information and felt that even if this woman was making this stuff up she was better than Einstein, Thoreau, William James and Sigmund Freud put together. What especially intrigued me was her continued reluctance to believe that Seth was who he claimed to be and her steadfast refusal to accept blindly this demonstration of reincarnation as well as the other material Seth conveyed.

Throughout the *SETH MATERIAL*, *Seth*, through Jane, introduces an entirely novel approach — extremely radical compared to traditional theories — on many subjects such as health, death, energy, time, GOD (Seth used the term *ALL THAT IS*), dreams and reincarnation.

The following are the basic tenets of Seth's philosophies:

1. *Every human being creates his/her reality.*
2. *Our thoughts, beliefs, emotions and expectations are projected out into the physical world.*
3. *There are no accidents nor coincidences.*
4. *All time exists simultaneously.*
5. *You may die in the Twentieth century and be reborn in the Seventeenth.*
6. *We choose our parents.*

7. *There are no victims.*
8. *Plants dream..*
9. *The point of power is in the present.*
10. *The universe is love, beauty, abundance, power, enjoyment, always for us, therefore, poverty, evil, sin, right and wrong are man-made.*
11. *Wars, violence, and diseases are caused by powerlessness.*
12. *We co-create the weather.*
13. *Each of us is a part of an over-soul or what Seth refers to as an entity that is composed of probable and reincarnated selves.*
14. *All of creaturehood including humans, plants, rocks, steel, trees and animals are vibrating units of consciousness consisting of electromagnetic energy that manifests itself from their inner selves to physical reality.*

For the next several years, I continued to be skeptical about reincarnation and who Seth claimed to be. I still could not accept the theory that any child or adult that happened to be killed or died from a disease actually attracted or chose that fate themselves. Nevertheless, it made me feel more comfortable that Seth encouraged his readers to be skeptical and to listen to the authority within themselves. In the ensuing years, I have explored these subjects and my observations of friends, co-workers and family have led me to firmly believe in *Seth's* teachings.

CHAPTER 2:
SPIRITUAL JOURNEY:
IMPLEMENTING THE MATERIAL

I had been researching the *SETH MATERIAL* extensively for approximately ten years, when I accepted the need to implement his philosophies into my day-to-day physical life. The more I taught group classes and individual sessions, the more I observed how we can indeed create our life through our beliefs.

I had my first successful experience in manifesting in 1978. My responsibilities as medical aide supervisor with the regional program for physically handicapped had expanded. Since I had significant academic and medical experience in the area of disabilities, I was asked to collaborate with Rich Locke, the transportation director, to help train his staff of special needs bus drivers and aides. Once we brought in an expert in the field of transporting special education students to talk to our drivers. This man had an excellent reputation and had written several articles about transporting the disabled. He charged $100.00 per day plus expenses. At that time in my life, $100.00 represented a lot of money. The presenter was good, extremely charismatic with vibrant energy. However his practical experience was limited and this became very evident to me as he presented his workshop.

Several days later, I approached Rich with the idea of collaborating to develop a workshop that we could conduct for our drivers, as well as other school districts. I told him we could do a better job than the "expert". Initially Rich was skeptical. *"But Ken, that guy has his masters and I only have a bachelor's degree, not to mention that although you have impressive actual experience you don't even have any degree."*

For the first time, I shared with Rich some of my metaphysical ideas. *"Rich, we create our reality according to our beliefs, therefore if we believe we can then indeed we can."*

Rich replied, *"Yes, but Ken, this consultant is well known and has published articles."* I responded with, *"Well, so can we!"*

Rich was willing to meet with me after work to talk about this idea of designing a workshop. He also urged me to share more about my philosophies. *"Rich, look around you. Everything around you — this glass, the table, everything outside — you actually see first from within through your thoughts. Everything invented starts out as an idea. First comes the idea, then words and then action. Everything is made of consciousness and each idea has its own electromagnetic energy that performs like a magnet attracting the corresponding desire. Therefore, like produces like. All of the events and experiences in our everyday life are first created in the form of blueprints in a sort of inner world. What we conceive with-in, we can create outside, or for, ourselves. Some people refer to this universal law as the law of manifestation: we are all the mirroring or out-picturing of our consciousness. And it is your beliefs and attitudes about yourself and life that dictate your consciousness."*

Spiritual Journey 17

This was to be Rich's first lesson in metaphysics. Then we began brain storming to develop our workshop. As we left the bar I said to Rich, *"Now the next step is for us to visualize ourselves doing this workshop and affirming the possibilities of school districts requesting our in-service program."* Much to Rich's surprise, several weeks later the Director of the Regional Program for the Physically Handicapped approached Rich with an inquiry. He had received a call from a school district in Northern Ohio looking for someone to conduct workshops for bus drivers who transport persons with disabilities. And he wanted to know if Rich was interested!

Rich was excited when he telephoned me to tell me about this unusual *co-incidence*. I explained to Rich that this was not a coincidence. It was the result of our combined effort to put our intent out to the universe and consequently life responded to our desires. Although Rich still considered what had transpired as coincidental, he nevertheless pursued the workshop idea with great enthusiasm, and when we had it completed he contacted the interested school official and scheduled our first workshop.

Then came the next major *co-incidence* to affect my life. At that time, my friend Jane Holder was seeing a psychologist to help treat her severe headaches. This therapist was teaching her how to release stress through relaxation exercises. Through the years, I had introduced Jane to the *SETH MATERIAL*, stressing how we create our own reality and there no victims. During a therapy session, Jane told the doctor about the *SETH MATERIAL* and expressed her feelings about how she was having difficulty with the concept that she may have drawn her illness to her. Her therapist insisted that she destroy this information and even suggested she limit, if not end, her relationship with the person who referred her to this garbage. One year later, this same therapist informed Jane that his associate, Dr. John Waddell, was going to be conducting classes on constructive thinking. I attended this weekly study group, and guess what text John utilized: the *SETH MATERIAL!* Jane confronted her former therapist, and he didn't even remember any conversation about the *SETH MATERIAL,* or any of the concepts Jane had discussed with him the previous year.

This was my first lesson that timing is crucial in determining whether or not someone is ready for a certain teacher, philosophy or event. Although at the time I realized that the *SETH MATERIAL* was not for everyone, I did learn that just because someone may not be ready for an idea at that moment, there may come a time later in their life when they will be more open to certain concepts.

I found the constructive thinking classes both interesting and stimulating. It was such a comfort to meet other people who not only had heard of the *SETH MATERIAL*, but also believed in the viability of the concepts. The *SETH MATERIAL* contained the most comprehensive philosophy I had ever read and the concepts just felt right to me. The more I studied it, the more each newly discovered thought, philosophy and emotion provided me with additional pieces to the puzzle of life. The *SETH MATERIAL* helped me put all of my existing pieces into a viable framework which allowed me to see what pieces I still needed to help create a beautiful, prosperous, safe, purposeful universe . . . a universe that we all *co-create.*

CHAPTER 3
LOOKING BACK:
Releasing My Dungeon Children

It was my original intent for this chapter to share some of the negative events I attracted in my past *only* to show you that no matter what conditions you choose in birth or co-create afterwards, it is still possible to transform your life if you are willing to change your thinking. However, when I sent a copy of this manuscript to my spirit teacher, Carin Waddell/*Haré*, I received some interesting feedback. They felt there was a need to review my feelings about my early life, especially my teenage years when I suffered so from an inferiority complex. They suggested I evaluate my life experiences with *"my intellect, emotion and intuition in harmony with each other."*

I took their advice and it was an interesting, emotional process, to say the least. As I reread the words describing my youth, I realized they were written by my ego/judgmental self instead of from a *feeling* level. As my spirit teacher stated, *"You have mis-judged the people and institutions and the rightness of their beliefs and why you drew them in. What feelings and beliefs were at work? What was learned? What was mirrored back?"*

I had to give that some thought. Was I still carrying around so much anger and resentment? And what was it doing to my health? *"You have given a perfect example of victimhood in your book. The institutions, as well as the different churches with its dogmas were created by all the peoples in this world and were valid at the time. They deserve our gratitude for their support and what we learned from them. The mass beliefs will be actualized and changed as new understanding sets in."*

Through the years, I have completed much of my self healing work, but now I know that to totally heal my current physical and emotional self, I must embrace and gently love and empower all of my past actualized and unactualized selves along with all the other people (friends and family), institutions and dogmas from my growing up years. I still have frightened, guilty, ashamed orphans that cower in the dark cellars of my past selves. A true spiritual awakening is all about shining a loving, non-judgmental, conscious spiritual flashlight gently upon these fearful children to help them out of their self-created fear and darkness into the light.

I once thought it wasn't necessary to go into your past to heal the present. I always believed that if you felt compelled to look back on your past, it was more beneficial to recall the positive memories and not to concentrate so much on past negative actions and history. I still think it is advantageous to remember the times you enjoyed or the experiences that made you feel the best. For example, if you grew up poor, remember when you received a gift, a raise or a Christmas meal and dwell in the memory of how those things made you feel rich. If you are feeling lonely or unloved, instead of recalling the heartbreak of divorce, or a broken or destructive relationship, help to transform your consciousness by remembering a positive relationship — even if it was with a cherished pet!

But I now believe that you must search through your past in a gentle, non-judgmental way, to empower, unconditionally love and accept those previously rejected, hurt, powerless, fearful children so you can accept and embrace all of you in the present moment. I only hope that this book will help you empower and release your neglected and abused past and present children from their inner dungeons.

My father was a buyer for boys' clothes at a prominent Dayton, Ohio department store. He met my mother there, they were married in 1947 and in the following year they received my sister Cherie into the world. They purchased a house in a middle-class white neighborhood. I chose my parents and decided to enter this reality on February 2, 1952, at 5:02 am.

As I've said, my mother had a difficult pregnancy with me. It was recommended she spend much of her time in bed with her legs elevated. The doctor continuously reminded her of the twins she lost before me, and warned her that the complicated pregnancy could result in a child born with significant physical or mental disabilities. Fortunately, although I was born with a learning disability, the results from a psychological evaluation showed that I was not mentally retarded. As the psychologist described it, my brain was like a busy switch board that sometimes had its wires short circuited. I received speech therapy and finally mastered my R's and was emancipated from special classes. It's ironic that although I wasn't born mentally disabled, much of my life would be devoted to empowering persons with disabilities, and even more ironic, even though I was born with speech problems I would eventually get paid to talk!

Once I overcame my speech problems, except for some minor respiratory problems I was pronounced basically *normal.* Of course over time we all would discover that I was really quite non-conventional — I had no desire to be a boring, *normal* person. Throughout my life I've been an extremely sensitive person and highly inquisitive. Although I have gained a lot of self-confidence, my early years were full of perpetual worry because I was so sensitive. I always worried about other people's feelings.

When I started kindergarten, Whittier School was 75% white. By the time I entered the second grade, it was 95% black. I developed my first significant friendship in the second grade with Robert (Nick) Williams, a boy who lived down the street from me. Nick was my size, but unlike me, he was very strong, coordinated and athletic. I could write an entire book on all the adventures Nick and I had throughout the sixties. Little could Nick and I know at the time of the challenges we would face to maintain our friendship, for I was white and Nick was black and we were entering the turbulent '60's when racism was pervasive.

At first, I didn't realize that I was "different" because by the time I was in the second grade, there were only two other white families in our school district and all of my friends were black. But then I began to be confronted with prejudice from the white world. My parents would take my brothers and I downtown to the Barber College where we could get a fifty cent haircut and I would listen as the barbers put down the local "niggers". And throughout my childhood I also remember a bigoted uncle talking about the "niggers." But I think the most frightening stories came from my elderly black neighbors who shared their experiences from their time down south, revealing horrors of verbal and physical abuse including witnessing a lynching. This began a period of questioning my self-worth and an identity crisis

Looking Back 23

that was devastating but would be the catalyst that gave me the opportunity to discover that although the world can be full of hate, tragedy, fear and violence, there is an internal life that we are connected with, always at our disposal, full of energy, peace and happiness that *can* be accepted and projected into our physical world.

My experiences put me in an awkward position — I was a white person prejudiced against *white people*. During the first twenty years of my life, I was made to feel very welcome by the Williams' family, as well another black family, the Townsend's. Rick Townsend (a genius according to our teachers) fulfilled my intellectual needs. In our elementary school days, he and I often competed for spelling contests and for the highest grades in class. I eventually introduced Nick to Rick and as we entered adolescence, our interests went from intellectual pursuits to alcohol and what was to become remembered as "our street days".

With the advent of the BLACK POWER movement in the mid and late sixties, I was no longer welcome outside of my immediate neighborhood. I was periodically beaten up by the blacks on our side of the river, and Nick and I were threatened whenever we crossed the river to the white side of town. I recall two vivid memories during the Dayton Race Riots of the summer of 1967. That summer I had a job at a paper stand in my neighborhood that started at 5:00 a.m. At the time, the National Guard had taken over several of the bars in volatile locations nearby. Early one morning they picked me up on my way to work and because I was white, they accused me of *being on the wrong side of town*. In addition to my paper route, I had a job as a janitor on the other side of town in a white suburb. As I was riding my bike back home, I was stopped by the National Guard who was refusing to allow whites across the bridge to the other side of town because they couldn't guarantee their safety. After convincing the guard that I did indeed live over the river they escorted me home.

For years, it seemed as though I didn't belong anywhere. And it only got worse. Events like these fueled my identify crisis: Am I white or black and where do I fit in? During that time I often thought of writing a book and calling it *IT SEEMS LIKE TWO WORLDS*. It seemed like I was living in two worlds because of the contrast between the two cultures. I felt like my life was in total confusion. Like a lot of other teenagers, I gave into peer pressure and started drinking and eventually suffered from this substance abuse.

My real test of survival came in 1966 when I graduated from eighth grade and moved on to Dunbar High School. Dunbar was named after Dayton's own Paul Lawrence Dunbar, the famous poet. This was primarily an all black, urban high school, except for the few white Appalachians who attended because they lived in a local slum in the district referred to as HOG BOTTOM. There were also poor blacks from this ghetto area, living in abandoned school buses or apartments like the one I visited where the bathroom waste fell directly into the basement.

At this new school, those black students who didn't know me from elementary school harassed me, calling me *Honky* and *Soda Cracker,* as well as throwing occasional punches to my chest. I decided enough was enough. I started to dress like the popular black dudes and hang out with the rough, tough crowd and became known as the *Blue Eyed Soul Brother Number 1*. My wardrobe consisted of alligator shoes and bright colored clothes, including neon orange and yellow suits I frequently borrowed from Nick. It would often freak Nick and Rick out when I would enter a bowling alley or a bar where whites were simply forbidden. I created such a powerful image that finally no one would mess with me *fearing* that I could really fight or *assuming* that I was probably carrying a gun. Although it was a convincing image, it was simply a front, because I've never been very physical. Instead I learned how to use human psychology to become a genius in the arena of street life.

My older sister ran away from home in 1966. At the time, she was involved with a black man who had embezzled money from a business liquidation deal with a local university. My sister, claiming to be in love with him, let him influence her and to her detriment this was the beginning of a lifestyle that would eventually lead to her death at the age of 45. Like so many people, especially some of the women I have known, she didn't know what love was and instead mistook love for need. This relationship resulted in a pregnancy that brought me my niece Paula. Since many of our friends were Black, having a bi-racial child in the family was accepted. But after Paula was born, my sister became involved with another man who exposed her to shooting up heroin, as well as cocaine, crack and a little bit of everything else. In order for her to afford her acquired habit she began to steal, forge checks and then became involved in prostitution. My parents, brothers, younger sister and I never accepted this lifestyle and attempted feverishly in vain to encourage her to abandon the hell she had created for herself. But after 20 years of shooting heroin and prostitution she died in April of 1994 at the age of 45.

I tell you my sister's story at this point for a reason. Halfway through high school, my family moved from our black neighborhood to an all-white neighborhood. I hated this move. I had finally been accepted at Dunbar High. In fact, I was even very popular. Belmont, my new high school, and my new "white world" seemed so foreign. On my first day at Belmont, the guidance counselor was surprised to find out I was white. She just assumed that I would be black since I has transferred from Dunbar. Even more amazing was the reaction of the basketball coach. When he heard that Belmont had a new transfer from Dunbar, he requested that I try out for basketball. Boy was he surprised when he discovered not only was I not black, but I was also far from being athletic. But the move was actually beneficial for my younger brothers, Tim and Tom, and for my younger sister Gloria, because it gave them the opportunity to grow up with, and get to know more white people which I believe lessened their propensity toward developing an identity crisis.

As for me, my reception at this new school was not good. The students made fun of my black accent and bright-colored, weird clothes and on many occasions I was chased home from school by students throwing stones and rocks. Once again I felt that in order to survive I had to resort to creating a tough posture. I purchased a switchblade and began to build another fearless image. But even as I did this, my *inferiority complex* continued to grow.

The most important reason for writing about these early stages in my life is to empower and give hope to any reader who was — or is now — in a similar place. No matter how troubled your life may be, I believe that by changing the way you think about yourself you can transform your life! When you love and believe in yourself, you will automatically interact with others harmoniously, contributing generously to society instead of draining its resources.

We have many probable selves and through our daily choices and decisions we choose which probable self to activate and consequently manifest in our outer world. In looking back, I now understand how that although my outer life exhibited pain, confusion and chaos, the periodic feelings of assurance I felt were emanating from my internal life. Eventually the concept that *you create your own reality* enabled me to overcome many of the challenges of my youth, and I manifested a completely different life from my brothers and sisters. Unfortunately my older sister was unaware of the many probable alternative realities she could have drawn in.

I developed an alcohol addiction and a massive inferiority complex that motivated me to do almost everything except for rape and murder. There where nights when I was so drunk that my bed would seem to spin out of control. Many of my friends ended up going to prison. One friend was sentenced to 10 to 25 years in prison for almost killing a gas station attendant during an armed robbery. Fortunately, I was not involved in that event! Ironically though, it was this person who turned me on to a book, *COMMENTARIES ON LIFE,* by Kristnamurti. This book inspired him to make some changes in his life while he was in prison.

Kristnamurti's basic theme encourages the individual to discount man-made authority and to learn to be free from the psychological structure of society. Emphasis is placed on listening to nature and becoming totally aware of self, others and the world without the influence of tradition and outside authorities. My friend used Krishnamurti's teachings to help him become more self-directed. As for me, it provided comfort and relief to know that many of the things I was feeling intuitively were also being contemplated by others.

It is fortunate that I have always been an extremely sensitive person and never wanted to hurt my parents, so my greater-self never attracted an event that might have led to a prison sentence. I could feel my *future-selves* reach for me with much compassion during the chapter of my insecure, street life. Gradually, I began to listen more and more to those wiser, powerful and gentler selves that began to provide me with guidance and direction in the form of intuitive messages.

Lydia was the object of my first infatuation. However, my first boy-girl relationship was based more on the physical passions of a lonely teenage boy. Lydia didn't satisfy my intellectual needs but I really enjoyed making out with her at every opportunity. However, this relationship stands out in my mind more for the insights it gave me into the social services and juvenile court system. Of course we are talking about the sixties and a time before the world was enlightened by the term *Dysfunctional Family*.

Lydia's father would come home drunk and curse up a storm and on many occasions he physically abused his wife and children. The most devastating and frightening experience involved Lydia's 6-month old baby brother. When her father's repeated attempts to get the infant to stop crying failed, he picked up the boy and literally threw him against the wall. Because of the constant abuse, Lydia would run away, only to be picked up by the police and placed in juvenile detention centers. Initially Lydia's response was probably the common sense thing to do to avoid verbal, physical and emotional abuse. But instead of addressing the root of her problem, which was her dysfunctional home life and chemically addicted and psychologically and physically abusive parent, the system punished Lydia for running away by incarcerating *her*. Lydia turned to her inmates at the juvenile detention centers to feed her hunger for acceptance. Her association with the troubled teens she met there led to a life of learning how to find acceptance among those peers by becoming a skilled criminal. Yes, on the streets those who don't receive approval and acceptances in a "socially acceptable way" often gain their self-esteem/self-worth by becoming the best thief, addict or fighter, being recognized accordingly by their fellow criminals.

This was the beginning of my realization that our so-called justice system is actually an *injustice* system. These life lessons provided me with an early understanding of the theory that *behavior is language*. Lydia's initial behavior of running away was a natural, normal response to her situation and should have been interpreted as a cry for help. Even today, society still uses punishment as a cure-all. But as I will explain in later chapters, punishment perpetuates the problem because it is an endless cycle: judgment creates guilt, guilt seeks punishment and punishment causes pain!

Lydia's story is a classic example of this cycle. At one point things got so bad for Lydia at home that I agreed to help her steal some wine from a store and sell it to other juveniles to provide her with enough money to run away for good. But the lessons she learned during her time spent in local juvenile detention centers didn't serve her well and she ended up at Marysville Correctional Center for Women. Several years later she tracked me down at a school where I was working, begging me to come back to her and even offering to be a prostitute for me. Since I had last seen her, I had grown so much in consciousness that it was no longer possible for me to relate to this woman. This saddened me, but at the same time it overwhelmed me to think about my transformation. I was no longer the same person I had been only five years before when I had first met Lydia. In retrospect, looking back at those years with Lydia, I know that my internal self often told me that my relationship with Lydia was only based on my inferiority complex, but my lessons learned regarding her dysfunctional family and the injustice system would assist my future self in becoming who I am.

Although in my younger days — or what I refer to as my *street days* — many of my friends were from "the other side of the tracks", I did have black friends that inspired me to pursue positive directions. During my early teenage years, I was introduced to culture and refined social graces through my childhood friend Steve Ward. My first exposure to classical music came as I listened to Steve's brother Kevin practicing on the piano. Kevin was a child prodigy, who began writing music as a young child. He studied at Julliard and later became a nationally recognized dancer. Even today my favorite classical piece is still Grieg's Piano Concerto in A Flat, a composition that Kevin played over and over for me at my request. What a contrast it was when I would go from playing with a friend in the impoverished part of the west side to stop off and visit my friend Steve and his family.

Although my experiences at my white high school gave me further reasons to be prejudice against white people, there were four students in particular that tried to comfort and welcome me: Roger Hummel, Phillip Andrews, Tom Cope and, of course, there was Bonnie Baer.

Roger and I shared choir classes and Phil and I were in the orchestra. Both were compassionate and went out of their way to help me fit in. Phil later became an attorney; Roger specialised in the communication business; and Tom became a policeman.

I also met Bonnie in choir and had a burning infatuation for her that lasted for several years. The incident that really sparked this feeling was the time that Bonnie helped Steve Ward and I take a group of black children from the elementary school I had attended on a camping trip. Not only did Bonnie prove to me she wasn't prejudiced, but her actions at the camp also made it apparent that she loved children and life in general. Unfortunately our relationship continued on a platonic level, but you can't say I didn't try. At that time in my life I had such an inferiority complex and I know I pushed too hard. But now I know that even if Bonnie had been interested in me intimately, I wouldn't have handled it right because deep down inside I didn't feel worthy or deserving. When I think about these special people and the time they spent in my life, I believe I can now recognize the pull of my future selves as they reached back to guide me, introducing me to people and events that would prepare me for my future.

CHAPTER 4
INTRO-SPECTION

The youthful chapter of my life ended when Nick William and Rick Townsend decided to enlist in the military. It was March 21, 1971 and the weather was beautiful so we decided to cruise to Cincinnati. Throughout our years together, the three of us would engage in philosophical conversations, as we drank our Budweiser. This first day of spring found us feeling extremely close to each other, with an intense affinity I will never forget. We sat beside a waterfall in a park and while we talked, as we had so many times before, we decided to call the day "Introspection Day". Although we had always enjoyed discussing philosophy, on that day we were deep into a conversation about a book entitled *SIDDHARTHA* by Hermann Hesse.

Hesse, a Nobel prize winning author, writes about his life-long examination of self-affirmation and spiritual quests that are in conflict with the social demands and beliefs of his culture. *SIDDHARTHA* is about a restless man who experiences worldly lust and greed while searching for the true purpose and meaning of life. Finally Siddhartha comes to a river where he finds peace, wisdom and finally true spirituality through nature.

Rick's girlfriend, Kathy Livingston, had introduced us to this book and other titles by Hesse. Kathy was a hippie, who introduced me to many of her like-minded friends. Conversations with these people stimulated my fervent desire to express ideas I had never before verbalized. I agreed with most of Kathy's ideas except for her belief in reincarnation. Nevertheless, *SIDDHARTHA* and other Hesse books like *KRISHNAMURTI*, instilled in me the self confidence to give credence to my inner messages. Not only could I relate to Siddhartha's spiritual quest, but it inspired me in my search for self-knowledge and more of life's experiences.

In retrospect, I find it fascinating that in March of 1971 I would have chosen the name *Introspection Day*. When I look back on our conversation from that day, I'm sure the self that's now writing *INTERNAL LIFE* was simultaneously reaching back, influencing the self that was that spring. *Introspection Day* was the last time Rick, Nick and I were together again, except for a brief encounter approximately ten years later when Rick's little boy died after being hit by a car.

While Rick and Nick went off to service, I found a job with Marshall's Fashions where the President/owner took me under his wing, training me to be a buyer. Mr. Marshall had high hopes that someday I would take over for him. I thought my life was set, but in 1971 my life's course was suddenly changed when I "won" the draft lottery. I came up with a low number. Although Kathy encouraged me to go to Canada and even introduced me to men who had deserted the army because of the experiences they had in Vietnam, I reluctantly chose to enlist in the Air Force. My experience at Lackland Air Force base during basic training was very traumatic for me. This nightmare brought to my consciousness everything I believed or *didn't* believe in. I felt like a character in a Hermann Hesse book. Oh, how I could identify with his characters' conflict of feelings.

Intro-Spection

The military is basically a paternal institution — do as you are told and you will do well. But I questioned everything from the mental conditioning to the purpose and ethics of our forces in Vietnam. In answer to each question I was told, *"Yours is not to ask the reason why, yours is to do or die."* Unfortunately, all the questions marked me as a troublemaker and turned the training instructors against me. The final showdown came when my dorm was assigned to guard a prisoner, an airman caught deserting, and we were ordered not to talk to him. Not only did I talk to this man, but he gave me a list of names and numbers of people in Canada that would assist me in the event I chose to go AWOL and defect. Like myself, this young man was sensitive and very intelligent — and it was hard for him to accept the brain washing or unquestioned conditioning. My interaction with the prisoner brought about severe repercussions and enhanced my adversarial relationship with my superiors.

I knew I had to get out of this rigid life style one way or the other. I took my concerns to my immediate superior but, of course, I got nowhere. I did find however that the higher I went on the chain of command the more educated and human I found the officers. I tried to get out on the basis of my severe acne condition, but the base doctors said that acne wouldn't make me eligible for a discharge. I did find a sympathetic ear, though. In fact, several of the doctors I spoke to admitted that the only reason they had enlisted was to get their education tuition and to place themselves in a better position to avoid being sent to Vietnam. Moreover, many actually voiced their resistance to an unjust and non-winnable war. Finally, I met a doctor who informed me that if I were to have an eczema outbreak *and* if I could get a dermatologist to document that I suffered from a chronic skin disease throughout my life, I would be eligible for an honorable discharge. As a matter of fact, I did have eczema as a child, so I wrote my parents asking them to request a letter from my childhood dermatologist.

Now, the next part of this story is the real reason for including this chapter of my life in *INTERNAL LIFE*. My training instructor discovered that I was trying to get a medical discharge and he became even harder on me, calling me "*a pussy*" as well as other names. From what I know now, I can understand that the Sergeant was doing the best he could. His position in the service allowed him in his own mind to *be somebody* and his mission was to turn boys into *real men*. Nevertheless, at the time I hated him and just as I was about to desert and go to Canada, my fingers started to break out in a rash. At the same time, I received a letter from my dermatologist stating that I had a history of chronic skin disease. This combination of events gave me my freedom! Not only was I free but I was able to gain my liberty without hurting my parents. I loved my parents and being sensitive to their opinions, I knew they wouldn't understand, let alone agree with my reasons for not wanting to serve in the military. After all, my father was a World War II veteran. It seemed like the best Christmas present ever when my father picked me up at the airport in Dayton, Ohio on Christmas Eve of 1971.

This was my first experience with the mind-body connection. While waiting for the dermatologist's response, I prayed every night that I would get whatever skin disease was necessary to provide me with a medical discharge. Of course, now I understand more fully that the sudden occurrence of the skin disease wasn't totally the result of prayer but of the mind/body connection which produced a metaphysical manifestation. This experience became an example I used many times later in my teaching. Certainly my rash was the product of stress, but it also was the end result of visualizing and concentrating to get what I wanted. And after all, doesn't that define prayer — asking the universe to respond to our requests through our thoughts, beliefs, faith and expectations?

When I returned from Lackland Air Force Base I wasn't satisfied with a future in the retail business, so I didn't go back to Marshall's Fashions. With nothing to occupy my time, I started to drink more than ever before. I spent more and more time in a place I came to consider as my personal sanctuary — a park high on a hill with a beautiful view of Dayton. At that point in my life I trusted nature more than people. I was tired of people with all their facades and games. Nature was real — no manipulation, no judgment and no masquerades. I began to develop a real affinity with nature and spent many introspective hours at Woodland cemetery, close to my home, and in the Fort Ancient area of southern Ohio.

In the park overlooking Dayton where I spent my time hugging the trees, I had the first "vision" or inner impulse that would prompt me along the road toward a life-long career. This vision involved walking with children in an old institution. My *little voice* suggested that I take a ride into the country. I left the park, but instead of taking my usual route on South Main towards Fort Ancient I headed off down North Main Street. As I left the city behind and drove further into the country, I came upon an old monstrosity of a building situated far off the main road. Was this the institution I had seen in my vision? I parked and entered the building. I was greeted by a nurse who thought I was there to volunteer on the children's floor. I hesitated and responded with, "*I'm here to learn more about what is involved in volunteering to know whether or not I'd be interested."*

As we toured the building, she explained that the first floor of the building was limited to tuberculosis patients. Initially the entire hospital had served as a tuberculosis sanitarium but with the decrease in TB cases, the county decided to use the facility to serve individuals with severe mental retardation and other medical and physical disabilities. She escorted me to the second floor where a young boy who walked with braces greeted me at the door. *"What is your name?"* he asked. The boy had spina bifida, but he seemed so happy and he was very verbal. But there were few other ambulatory residents, as most of the people I observed were severely retarded and confined to bed.

The volunteer coordinator took me on a tour that would have a tremendous impact on my emotions and would change my life forever. There were people in this institution with conditions that I never knew existed: an individual with Hydrocephalus whose head was literally larger than his body; children with deformities beyond your imagination caused by mutations from German measles and various drugs, both legal and illegal; and more common disabling conditions such as cerebral palsy and mental retardation.

As I toured the facility, I kept asking myself, *"If there is a God, then why would he allow poor innocent children to be born this way?"* I felt sick to my stomach and didn't see how anyone could ever work with these people. At the end of the tour, the volunteer coordinator encouraged me to return and volunteer. I left that place that smelled of urine and bowel movements with no intention of ever returning. I returned to the park to my tree friends where I had found peace in solitude. I drank myself into oblivion as I cursed God and wondered if there really was such a caring

Intro-Spection

deity. But a few weeks later I did return to Stillwater Health Center. I finally accepted my inner guidance that kept insisting I create a new chapter in my life.

In those early days at Stillwater, volunteers were mostly used to assist nurses and aides in bathing, feeding and dressing those children with severe disabilities. In addition, we attended to several adults who had contracted spinal meningitis. They would just lie in their beds and stare into space, as if their souls/personalities had left their bodies.

I was still saddened by the things I saw, but something strange was happening to me. Several weeks had passed and guess what — I was still volunteering. Over the course of time, several of the volunteers and I instituted a physical therapy and education program at Stillwater. Although years later a federal law was passed that guarantees all children a right to an education, at the time, the children at this facility were still spending their entire day in bed. The needs of these children were beyond comprehension and the progress we made with each child was slow, but the results were rewarding. It was so fulfilling to see how I could improve the lives of others that I started to volunteer at least 60 hours per week. It took me two hours a day, seven days a week for four months to teach one young girl how to grasp a spoon and bring it to her mouth to feed herself. And I spent a similar amount of time helping one boy to maintain his balance until he could take several steps. WOW! I had patience and perseverance that I had no idea I possessed.

And there was so much else to do. I especially enjoyed the experience of training other volunteers. My time at Stillwater did more to build my self-esteem then anything I had previously experienced. Not only did I feel better about myself, but I finally had a sense of purpose. I spent less time drinking and rarely saw old friends from my "inferiority" days. However, my savings was running low and although I know my father did so with the best of intentions, he started to lecture me, saying, *"I know you love those kids but you can't live on love."* At the time I agreed that he was right, but little did I know that a quarter of a century later I would conduct workshops about doing what you love, and loving your job and it will take care of you. Yes, most people would have agreed with my father, but neither he nor I realized that the time I was investing at Stillwater was much like going to college. I gained experience and developed a passion that would later help me in my career in the field of caring for people with disabilities.

During my time at Stillwater I discovered the importance of finding a purpose in life, especially when it amounts to something of value for others as will as yourself. This was one of the first major steps in my self-rehabilitation process. Later this sense of purpose, combined with my belief work from the *SETH MATERIAL*, would help me learn to live the life I was meant to enjoy. My experience at Stillwater illustrates how our intuition constantly gives us insights and directions. But we have to pay attention. And most important, we have to feel when the timing is right to act upon these urges and respond to this inner guidance.

Think back on your life and see if you can recall a period when you followed your "little voice" and the subsequent changes it brought to your life. You may also remember an undesirable event in your life that may have been avoided if you had acted upon those impulses that were trying to warn you. List what seems like any coincidences that occurred throughout your life. Eventually you will discover that those "chance meetings" or accidents were merely synchronicity — being at the right place, doing the appropriate thing in order to create an event or experience that you either desired or believed possible. At the same time, begin to note any new *co-incidences* that happen. As you become more aware, this will help you make beneficial choices that can result in desired *future* events and opportunities.

❖ ❖ DAD ❖ ❖

Clearly my finding Stillwater was no accident, for not only did it lead me into the field of dealing with people with disabilities, but it helped me establish a close bond of unconditional love and acceptance with my father when he became disabled.

Diabetes runs in my father's family. My dad's two aunts lost both their legs to the disease and my grandmother lost her eyesight and died at an early age in the county nursing home that was referred to as "the poor house." My paternal grandfather died the same year. My dad was passed from one relative to another and finally, his family persuaded him to lie about his age in order to join the Army.

My mom also had an unstable childhood. Her father was a senior citizen when she was born. He had a diverse work career, ranging from owning a farm to delivering the mail . My mother's sister was much older then her. She was already married and living in Dayton when my mother was just a child. My grandmother died when my mother was eleven and she was forced to leave rural, southeast Ohio and move in with her sister.

Because my parents regretted having lost their childhood years, they were committed to making the best possible life for their children. For most of his working career my father worked two jobs and since he was away from the house so much, I spent more time with my mom and never really got to know my father. Although my mom was receptive to esoteric philosophies, my dad thought any thinking that was not in the traditional vein was merely *nuts*. This included any form of counseling or psychology. Then in 1974, he lost a leg to diabetes. A few years later in 1977, he had a major stroke that left him paralyzed on one side for a while. It was during this time that I became extremely close to my dad. At first I didn't know what to say or how to respond to his grief and despondency over his disabilities. My dad grew up with the idea that a man is judged by how strong he is and on his ability to stand on his *own* two feet. At first, he felt the loss of his leg and the stroke that resulted in some upper body limitations was symbolic of his loss of manhood. But as I spent more and more time with him during this period in his life, he gradually revealed a beautiful, sensitive side of himself I had never seen. Soon after his stroke, he confessed to me that he always got teary eyed whenever he saw anyone, whether in real life or even on TV, get hurt or express displeasure. Over the next few months, I grew to love this part of my father; this unwavering concern and a selfless giving to the people he loved, even though he was suffering himself. It was this unconditional love and acceptance of others that influenced me to become unconditional in *my* love and acceptance of others.

CHAPTER 5
NEW REALITIES:
Do I Believe in Ghosts?

My initial introduction to the *SETH MATERIAL* brought on an insatiable urge to study and read more. I never believed in spirits or reincarnation and I was extremely skeptical about the source of this material, nevertheless the more I read, the more the information made sense to me. Intuitively, I began to feel *right* about these concepts. It was as if I had begun to put some very crucial pieces into the puzzle of my life. The *SETH MATERIAL* provided me with the most comprehensive explanation about the nature of personal reality, as well as the nature of the multidimensional universe. The essence of the *SETH MATERIAL* is the message that *you create your own reality*. I believe this one concept, once recognized and accepted universally will transform science, religion, medicine, politics, psychology, philosophy, education and business. In fact, when I conduct seminars on prosperity I attract business officials and people who are sometimes conservative and I use this concept as their introduction to esoteric metaphysics.

But I'm getting ahead of myself. . .

Let me return to the evolution of my spiritual growth. In 1977, I began taking constructive thinking classes from Dr. John Waddell in Yellow Springs, Ohio, a town not far from where I lived. After a year of these group classes, John explained that although he was using the *SETH MATERIAL* as the text, he was being guided by his own spiritual teacher, an entity that is referred to as *Haré*. During one class, John introduced us to his mother, Carin Waddell, who taught constructive thinking classes in Pittsburgh, Ohio. She talked to us about her life in Germany and her move to America. Most intriguing were her stories about how *she* first consciously connected with *Haré*, an energy-essence personality like *Seth*. After listening to Carin speak, I knew that I wanted to study with her. She suggested I either spend some time with her in Pittsburgh during the summer, or make the long trip to Pittsburgh for one weekend a month. Months past and although my interest in calling Carin in Pittsburgh was intense, for some reason I just kept putting the call off. This was unusual because even though I procrastinated in some areas of my life, when it came to metaphysics I could hardly wait to study something new. To discover a new *Seth* book on the bookstore shelf brought forth joyous emotions. It made me feel like a child again opening presents on Christmas morning.

Once again another *co-incidence* proved that there was a reason and purpose for everything in my life, even the procrastination! The day I decided to call Carin to make plans to travel from Dayton to Pittsburgh, I got a phone call from John Waddell. He was calling to tell me his father had died and that his mother was moving to Yellow Springs. She was planning to offer individual classes and he was calling to see if I would be interested in studying with his mother. Of course, I said yes, but not before telling him about the "coincidental" timing of his phone call.

New Realities

Classes with Carin were stimulating and challenging. I was especially intrigued when Carin would talk to her spiritual guide, the entity *Haré*, as if he was physically present in the room. Carin Waddell grew up in Germany, and still spoke with a heavy German accent. Living through the Nazi Germany years, she was aware of how collective beliefs create reality and how the fanaticism of a leader like Hitler could destroy nations. Because of the paranoia that existed during World War II in Germany, Carin initiated her spiritual work with caution. When she moved to Pittsburgh, she developed a relationship with Diane, who eventually became her psychic secretary. Diane would receive automatic writing from *Haré*, Carin's spiritual teacher. By the time I met Carin she was receiving messages directly from her guide. With Carin's help, I discovered that *Haré* was also assisting me.

In the seventies, channeling was not yet well received, so when Jane Roberts started speaking for *Seth* in 1963 it was considered by some as a rare gift and by others as a hoax. In my sessions during the seventies, *Haré* informed me that the eighties would find many of his associates revealing themselves in order to assist us in consciously creating a reality of choice. *Haré's* predictions have come true, as I myself have become aware of more than one hundred energy essence personalities over the last decade.

While teaching her classes in Yellow Springs, at least two of Carin's other students started to receive dictation from *Haré*. My favorite part of each session with Carin was receiving and reviewing new dictation. The subject matter ranged from scientific, health, physics and psychology to spirituality and reincarnation! Although at first I was still skeptical, it didn't take me long to acknowledge and accept the source of the automatic writing because no matter which new student received the dictation, the style and content was consistent with *Haré's*. It was even more exciting and amazing to discover that the same entity was corresponding with other people I met as I traveled around the country.

After several years of classes with Carin and *Haré*, they encouraged me to start teaching my own students. I was reluctant to teach at first because although I had come to accept that teaching/facilitating was one of my primary purposes for this lifetime, I didn't feel qualified because my life didn't reflect my new beliefs yet. But my teachers knew I was ready and convinced me that I would simultaneously transform *my* consciousness as I helped others to identify and transform *their* beliefs. Once I accepted the challenge, I wasn't sure how to go about getting students. *Haré* reminded me of the old sage's message, *"When the student's ready the teacher will appear."* He encouraged me to believe that the opposite applied too. *"When the teacher is ready the students will appear."*

Once again, I found a synchronicity of events changing my life. In the past I had attended several inspirational lectures by Elizabeth Kelly, a prominent, well-respected spiritual teacher and psychic who lived in Yellow Springs, Ohio. During these sessions I had an opportunity to share with her my interest in the *SETH MATERIAL*. Soon after I had decided to start my spiritual teaching, I went to Liz and before she started my reading she surprised me by asking if I was still studying the *SETH MATERIAL* and if I conducted classes. Clients of hers, Gwen Elam and her sister, Sharon Barton, had expressed interest in learning more about the *Seth* concepts and how to implement them into their daily lives. Liz remembered my interest in the *SETH MATERIAL* and wondered whether or not I would be interested in giving some classes. She gave me their number and shortly afterwards I held my first class. These weekly classes, held at Gwen's home or Sharon's, lasted for years as the group grew to include some of their friends, relatives, work associates and neighbors.

One topic we discussed often was how wonderful it would have been to learn these concepts when we were children so we would not have to *unlearn* so much as grown-ups. Those discussions were the catalyst for developing classes for children. In these classes, I worked with the children on developing their psychic powers, enhancing self-esteem and using more of their imagination and creativity. Gwen and Sharon's children were the first members of this class and soon other members of my adult class started bringing their children as well.

At the same time I was teaching *Seth* classes for Gwen and Sharon and their friends, I would periodically teach a class in the Mountain Top Book Store in Dayton. A friend of mine, Bob Hardman, who was a pediatric neurologist, brought his wife Sally to one of my classes at the book store.

Not only was Sally interested in *Seth* and other similar philosophies, but she also received information from my spiritual teacher *Haré*. Soon after our meeting, Bob and Sally were divorced and Sally moved to Ft. Lauderdale, Florida. However, Bob and I remained close. Like Bob, I was grieving over the loss of a relationship. During this period Bob and I found comfort and fellowship at the Unity Church of Dayton. Then one week in the spring of 1981, Bob met a lovely lady named Kate. They were married later that year. The same week, because I listened to my inner voice, I too met the woman whose love I now share.

For two years, people at work kept asking me to go to one certain club in town to party with them. Suddenly, one Friday evening I decided to go. On my way to the club, I stopped by my parents' house to say hello. My mom was working and my father seemed lonely so I decided to stay with him instead of going on to the club. However, I had an intense impulse to go to this club. My little voice won out and a while later I left my dad and headed out. At the same time, Leslie Stewart was deciding whether or not she really wanted to make the forty-five minute drive from her hometown in Sidney, Ohio to some club just south of Dayton. But she also had an inner prompting to go. One of the common threads running throughout the *SETH MATERIAL* and then emphasized in the automatic writing from my teachers during that period of my life was the importance of following my impulses and being spontaneous. Too often we limit ourselves to certain routines and rituals that keep us stuck in the familiar and prevent us from enjoying life's surprises. Leslie and I are both grateful that we listened to our inner guidance as we continue to share our life and our love.

The information I was receiving from these ghosts, spirits, entities or whatever they wish to be called, was beginning to make more and more sense to me both intuitively and logically. When I first started to study the *SETH MATERIAL*, I wasn't sure if I believed that *Seth* was who, or what, he claimed to be. But after time, that no longer mattered because as I came to appreciate the value of the information, the source *itself* no longer mattered. Still, I began to develop a strong appreciation for *Seth* and then *Haré* and the apparent network of spirits all working to assist us from the *other side*. I began to believe that maybe

New Realities

Casper wasn't alone — maybe there are lots of friendly ghosts!

In fact, I have often wondered if we are looking in the wrong direction with our space program, searching for aliens and the origins and purpose of the universe. More and more I'm convinced that the answers about the universe are within each of us. Gradually more humans will experience entities/spiritual beings like *Haré* and come to their own conclusion that we are not alone in the world. *THEY* ARE HERE! They are not invasive; they reveal themselves through our permission only; and they don't have to be unidentifiable (UFO's) if we would only try to allow them to identify themselves. More important, we will realize that they are not really *alien* or separate from us, but merely connecting with us from a different dimension where we all exist in **INTERNAL LIFE!**

CHAPTER 6
MEETING *AMEL*:
I Do Believe In Spirits

In the spring of 1981, I was holding weekly classes at my apartment. During one session, we were working on how to become more spontaneous and trust our inner impulses. One of my students wanted to share an experience she had during the previous weekend. She told us about a channeling session she attended called a "trance circle". She asked if I was interested in attending a future session. Being the skeptic that I was, I initially expressed a reluctance to attend, using as my excuse that fakes are common in the field of the paranormal. But the class ganged up on me! *"Wait a minute. You were just talking about being spontaneous and following your impulses,"* they all cried. They were right. Instead of being rigid and judging someone I had never met, I suggested that the whole class go together and we could all make our own determinations about a trance circle.

The others agreed and the student made arrangements for our class to have a private session with the channeler. The channeler introduced himself as Rev. Gordon Stonehouse. By that time, I was already so disillusioned with organized religion that just his title of reverend alone made me very skeptical of Gordon's abilities. He explained what the session would involve: the first part of the session would consist of a lecture from an entity by the name of *Amel*, after the lecture he would respond to questions about what he refers to as his "commercial" or any inquiry of a general nature; during the next part of the trance circle each person could ask personal questions; and finally, after each participant exhausted their personal questions, *Amel* would accept any other questions we might have forgotten to ask. We all agreed we understood and the session got underway.

Gordon removed his glasses, closed his eyes and said a prayer. Then, after a short pause, he began to speak in a booming, forceful voice with a unique foreign accent. This voice was extremely different from Gordon's and even his facial features changed as he began his lecture. My initial skepticism faded as *Amel* began to discuss simultaneous time. To that date, *Seth* was the only resource I had read that portrayed reincarnation in that fashion, and we used Seth's references in class all the time. *Amel's* mention of simultaneous time brought smiles to our faces and put us all at ease.

From then on, we all listened with rapt attention and waited eagerly for the time when we could ask our personal questions. No person could have faked the insights and knowledge *Amel* had as he answered each of us. Little did I know at that time that Gordon and I would become close friends and I would experience well over one hundred sessions with *Amel*.

I would like to share with you the commercial (lecture) given by *Amel*:

I am very pleased to have this opportunity to express the sensitivity of this one so that I can converse with you in a way that will be both intelligent to you and of practical benefit to you in your continuing quest for greater realization of those things of the soul self which allow you to fulfill the will of your heavenly father and to live a long and good life upon the earth as we come together this day. It is as always in recognition and in acceptance of the one power, and the one presence throughout the universe, god, the good, the omnipotent and understood that we are each one now the full and complete expression of that power and presence that we are now in the intelligence of the divine self - expressing itself in each of us as me. We come together this day, not because we have been lead to believe that there is one accessible to us who knows more and understands more and can do more than any of us are able to do. We have not come here because someone has convincingly sold us of the value and benefit of meeting together in this way. We have not come here to receive a letter-perfect definition of ourselves and an accurate and complete lifetime portrayal of all that we will encounter upon the earth plane.

We have come here out of an all consuming desire to know and to be ourselves. To express fully all of the ability which we possess; to understand and to accept and express in harmony's ways, which will not only be a blessing to ourselves but to all we may meet along life's way; to express the gifts of mind, heart and hands. Because we know that we have not yet fully developed or excavated that region of ability that lies inherent within us, we avail ourselves of opportunities such as this which we are enjoying at this time, because we are determined to be fully alive and completely expressing the light, the love, the intelligence and the life which we are.

INTERNAL LIFE

In coming to you this day, I have made the choice to share with you my being, my knowledge and my desire to recruit from you what out of your experience in life I can use to continue my own development and contribute to my greater advancement. I have not come to you because it is part of my sentence to do service to atone for past sins or to pay off some debt. I have not been given a suspended sentence, placed on probation and required to do "X" number of hours of community service-type work to justify my right to live. As this is true for me, so it is true for each one of you. That you have chosen to be here in this place - that you have responded to the invitation that life has given to you to better acquaint yourself with yourself. You have discriminated against all other possibilities that you could have participated in this day, in order to be here - and being here you are saying to yourself that you are worthy of the best, you deserve the best - that you expect the best and that you will only accept the best! You may feel inclined to disagree, to argue with me, but that part of your multidimensional self which wants to argue and contest the point is a fabrication of the societal influences to which you have been subjected. It does not originate, nor is it endorsed or approved of by the true self, the soul self. But a soul self is always saying yes too good. It is always saying yes to growth. It is always saying yes to enjoyment. It is always saying yes to the challenge to demonstrate what it is and what it can do. You are, much to your consternation, logically a "yes" creature. As the chairman of the board says we are going to do that, you automatically nod your head and say yes or you jump up and say Amen. You cannot help yourself, for you are under a divine implosion to radiate and to express completely that quality of self which is absolutely and eternally your nature: to be loving, to be creative, to be constructive, to be in a state of harmony; to experience abundant well being and to enjoy radiant physical well being; to have wisdom to be filled with true understanding and insight; and to enjoy the grand and wonderful adventure called life. The difficulties which you encounter, the trials and tribulations which frustrate and perplex you, are the results of resisting yourself and attempting to deny yourself and to prevent yourself from having what is your right. It is the will of your creator that you have not in a fleeting way not just a scent of it - a lick of it or a little crumb - but to gorge yourself, to glut yourself, to so fill yourself of all the good and to do so as often as you have the desire or the inclination to pig out. From the divine food you cannot get hummungus - a gigantic being wondering where your feet are because the mid-region sticks out so far you don't know whether you have or don't have feet anymore. Enjoy the good which is continually being created for you! God does not need it! It is created for you. As much as you take, as much as you utilize it, as much as you apply it, there is that much more to be applied, to be utilized, to be taken, to be accepted, to be enjoyed. This, my friend of the earth life, is what immortality, what eternity is all about. You (we) are not expected to take that which we don't like - that which we don't understand, that which we cannot apply, that which won't help us to be more loving, more tolerant, more understanding, more accepting, more responsive, more expressive, more enjoying. When you go to the most acclaimed eating establishment in your world, you may even happen upon a smorgasbord of such delectable delicacies that you are drooling, slobbering all over yourself before you even get your plate and begin to fill it. You will take some of each from that array of beautiful and delectable dishes, but only what you enjoy. If you get lots of beans and wieners at home you are not going to eat beans and wieners. You are going to enjoy - not to the point that you make yourself sick - but to the point of satisfying yourself. You are going to partake of the caviar, the champagne. Or if this is what you have all the time at home, you will enjoy the beans and wieners. You will take that which will enable and allow you to be the well-adjusted rounded soul, the harmonious, contended, creative, constructive, joy-filled, loving and positive being that you are assigned to be and that you are supported to be by all the power and all the resources in the cosmos, in the universe, in the world, in the mind, in the reality of your own experiences. If you have less of this goodness in your life than another, it is not because you are less deserving, it is not because you are like a pimple on the ass of God and irritation to God and therefore punished. It is because you do not see yourself as deserving, or able to use, or enjoy, or appreciate these things. It may be because you are afraid that if you had that Lamborghini you desire you wouldn't be able to enjoy it. You would be worrying each time you park it: what if someone, somebody steals it. You would be thinking what would people think, what business does he have? Or who does she think she is driving around in a Lamborghini, when I have to drive around in my Volkswagen, which is falling apart? Or I have to peddle my ass all over town upon this bicycle. These are the types of things which impede your progress and prevent the establishment in your life of that abundant prosperity. That is the will of your father/mother god - that you

Meeting *Amel*   57

enjoy. Not occasionally, not most of the time - but all of the time. And for that one or two of you who may not understand what the word "All" means, I will define it for you - hopefully in terms that you can readily accept and understand. All means without exceptions, without limitations. It is not like a law, enacted by a legislative body in your world that says this is what will happen except for so on and so forth and this and that one. There are no exceptions to what all of the time means. The difficulty is that your concept of prosperity is confined to money - to things. It does not include health, happiness fulfilling relationships, right employment of your talents or living in the environment that is most harmonious for you engaged in the activities that best allow you to express the gift of mind, heart and hands.

You are not a pebble that must stay where it has been put by the motion of the waves beating upon the shore, or where some child has flung you, or where some animals push you. You are self determining, self knowing, self actualizing, self realizing and self limiting creatures. If you don't like where you are and what you have, don't blame god, don't blame those around you, don't even blame yourself, for blame will perpetuate the gestation. Look to see in yourself what it is of your belief about self and your relationship to life, what it is about your memory that you cling or give to yourself; what it is about your dreams, your goals, your desires, your sense of your purpose in life that has drawn this situation to you and makes you sit as one immobilized by fear - waiting for the gator to munch on you and to enjoy the tidbits that you are to it. Life is not some gator who has lived a hundred years in the canal that you happened to go swimming in today. Life is supporting you - expressing itself in you - as you! It is not in competition with you, it is not opposing or obstructing you. It is at all times, in all places, in all conditions, under all circumstances, lovingly holding you in its palm, nurturing, warming, strengthening, uplifting, enlightening and enabling you. No matter how little or how much may be the gift of life to you, you will only have that much that you are willing to accept; that much that you believe you deserve and can use; that much that you feel that you can be responsible for; that much that you envision yourself being able to enjoy. And so my friends of the earth life, your test, your work, your job today as it has always been, as it shall always be - your job is to enlarge your consciousness. To give up your attempt to paint a miniature and to put into place the biggest piece of canvas you can unfold and to get the biggest candle to illumine that space so you can see what you're doing and to paint a panorama - not a little miniature that you have to take a magnifying lens to the hundredth power to even see, to get a general idea what is in that pinhead of consciousness that you've been painting on. Go out on the sky of consciousness and if you want to paint the town red, do so. But don't complain if instead of red you paint it black and blue and gray all over, and you find yourself nauseous to the point that nothing and no one is of any interest or appeal or any excitement to you. Accept what is your right, your duty - to be responsible and to know your responsibility is eternal. Never have you had, never will you have, never can you have a time when your ability to respond is taken from you. Always, my friend of the earth life, there is at least a choice between two things that you can make. Even if it is simply to choose to be accepting or to reject or to make the most of what you have or to feel sorry for yourself because you have so little. It is, as it always has been, as it shall always be, that the life that you make for yourself is either one of happiness or unhappiness, of fortune or misfortune, of health or of disease, of accomplishment or of failure. That your life epitomizes and represents and signifies at this time, a result of your choice and your acceptance of beliefs and ideals and memories and observations and criticisms of others. You are indeed in the state of sin. You have subjected and continue to subject yourself to sin - to self-inflicted nonsense that prevents you from enjoying the garden of delights which your father/mother god has given to you and gives, and gives. It is a little early for Christmas, but I do not think that it is too early . . . to give a present to yourself; to make to yourself an offering of this moment. To give yourself now an opportunity to enjoy, to experience, to express all of the intelligence, all the life, all the love, all the life that you are aware of. In this sense everyday is a Christmas, and the stocking of your consciousness should be filled to overflowing with the image and the desire and the expectation of good, not only for yourself, but for all that you encounter upon your pursuit of life. There is strength and there is peace, there is courage and there is confidence, there is skill and there is application of that skill. To the words that I have been able to share with you this day, I add the blessing of my own small measure of knowledge, understanding, love and acceptance. I wish that you may find an intensification of the peace within your heart, in your mind and in your soul, and that that peace will be a daily occurrence.

Now I give to you an opportunity to ask the questions that have come to your mind as a result of what I have been able to share with you thus far, utilizing the sensitivity of this one who has voluntarily placed himself at our disposal, yours and mine, so that we can converse together in an intelligent and practical way. I ask of you only two things: one, that you will not all speak at once. Although it may not be important to you what another has to say, it is important to me and I do not wish to miss one word of what you have to say. And the second thing I ask of you is that you will not all sit on ceremony waiting for someone else to go first because you think your question is not important enough or not expressed perfect enough. If it means enough for you to ask it, it means enough to me to give you the very best answer I possibly can. So who will be the brave one to go first today with a question arrived from what I've been able to share with you this far?

Question: You mentioned that we should live to experience all the good things.

Amel: That's all there is to experience. That which you call bad is your refusal, your resistance to experiencing good.

Question: Will this help us? How will this help?

Amel: If it wouldn't help out I wouldn't be wasting my time talking about something that isn't obtainable. I have better things to do on such a beautiful afternoon and certainly my instrument would enjoy going to the beach and watching the visual delights that are to be

	found there! What you do with it is up to you, my friend of the earth life.
Person:	I understand - what I mean is, how does it help us when we reach the end of this life? Are there certain levels?
Amel:	It is not a question of how does it help us when we reach the end of this life. It is a question of how is it helping me now to live life fully, to live completely a life of quality and to have content in my life that is to my satisfaction. As we live here today, so we will live here after. No? And if today we are in harmony then, we are in the state of balance. We are not self centered to the point we are oblivious to the needs and gifts that others can make to us. No matter what dimensions we enter into, we will be able to function in a healthy, positive, prosperous way. No? I don't pray today because tomorrow when I get to the proverbial gate Peter will say "Yes down there you were a good friend. You must have been a very righteous and holy person, you spend a lot of time praying."
Question:	Is it not true we are judged by are deeds?
Amel:	That judgment that is paid is what you are. When you take any one sample to the assay office the assayer doesn't judge it on the size of it. It goes to work on it to extract the various minerals that are in it and gives you a report as to the likely value of that ore per

	ton. Do you understand?
Person:	Yes - You are what you are.
Amel:	EXACTLY! And what you are doesn't need an explanation. And only a fool would try to explain what he is because no one can understand what another is. They can only understand what they themselves are. You understand?
Person:	Yes - Does this also take place on your side?
Amel:	Exactly, We know, we are known, as we know.

Meeting *Amel* 63

The personal question and answer segments of *Amel's* trance circles were always very exciting for me. During the first few sessions I attended, *Amel* provided me with confirmation of my budding feelings and passions. He said I would become a lecturer and a teacher and that I would become involved in the healing process of individuals by assisting in the transformation of their consciousness. I was really surprised the first time he referred to me as *"a drunken monkey"* and *"a pickled Herring"*. In his own way, with symbolic words, he was saying if I wanted to make my dreams a reality and if I wanted to continue living, I'd better either moderate my alcohol consumption or eliminate it completely. WOW! How did he know I liked my beer? Although by 1981 I was drinking much less then during my inferiority days, I would often still drink to excess over the weekends. Instead of immediately heeding *Amel's* message though, I went out and got plastered! Still I was amazed at how beings in other dimensions can be so aware of the happenings in our focused reality.

On one of my first dates with Leslie, I revealed to her that I talked with spirits, or what many people would think of as ghosts. She was open to learning more about this ability and she became a regular participant of Gordon's trance circles. Now she also had the opportunity to converse with spirits.

The following is one of *Amel's* lectures Leslie and I shared.

Amel Session: 1-25-85

I am very pleased to have this opportunity to utilize the sensitivity of this one so that I can converse with you in a way which will be both intelligent to you and of practical benefit to you in your continuing quest for greater utilization of these things of the soul self to allow you to fulfill your will of the heavenly father and to live a long and good life upon the earth plane.

As we come together this day, it is as always in recognition and in acceptance of the one power and the one presence throughout the universe - god, the good, the omnipotent - understanding that we are now each one the whole, complete and perfect manifestation of that power and presence which reveals itself in and through each one of us as an ineffable life and exsorable love and inexhaustible life. In coming together, we have the opportunity to learn one from the other, for our consciousness is merging into a great pool of creativity and our strength causes a great power to be distributed from one to the other, balancing, harmonizing, stabilizing, uplifting, illuminating each one of us. We are all partaking of that which each of us is. We are each being affected by what the other is, aspiring to do and to become. And to the extent that we are in harmony with ourselves and with life, we will experience that which is called negative and positive in such a way that it will not disrupt our equilibrium by either down-grading our quality of our conscious thoughts or by so up-grading it that we are temporally unable to deal with the effect.

We are all the time a filter system, extracting what we are exposed to from that which we can use. And if we are in understanding of self, totally accepting and not frightened by those areas that are not yet as well illuminated as others we will know, then there is nothing in another that can disrupt our equilibrium or create for us disease or distress or adverse conditions of any kind. The only one who can cause these difficulties is myself and only then to the extent that I am unwilling to learn about the power and the ability which is mine and mine alone to use. So many in your world have not been encouraged to think for themselves, to explore and experience life for themselves and to acquaint themselves with the power and majesty of life that is in all people, in all things, in all places. This path of discovery has been foreclosed to many people in your world because they have not received an example that allows them to know that they can depend upon self and that the more they experience, express and ENJOY that self, the more confidence, skill and ability they will have at their disposal to create for themselves a world of harmony, peace, beauty, tranquillity and abundance in every imaginable form, to an extent that would frustrate the most efficient of the auditors from the Internal Revenue Service.

We are indeed our own auditor in this internal revenue service. Unlike the earth realm where you have a taxation period come due once a year, in the development of your intellect, your emotions, your physical body and your soul self you are in need of constant attention to that which you amass, either assets or liabilities. Do not let one day pass where there is not a balance between the assets and liabilities which either inhibit or restrain the progress of the soul. We have come each one . . . out of the unknowing into the knowing, to express that which we are. All that we do allows us to be more aware and to demonstrate to a *greater degree than we have ever done before, the talent and ability which make us what we are. So often in your world you refer to talent as ability and ability as something which you have, rather than as something which you are.*

You do not possess life, you are life possessing itself.

You are light. . . you do not have light. . . you are light and that light is not intermittently cast out into the darkness of unknowing.

It is continually pulsating and enlightening all the regions of consciousness. . .

You are not possessing love, you are love, always expressed with increased intensity. . . LOVE UNCONDITIONAL!

You do not have life - you are life - expressing itself fully even at those times when you believe that you have completely shut yourself off from contact with those others in your world and from the world itself. Even in the darkest place in which you hide for a time, life is there fully revealing itself in and through you, as you. Not even if you were to create for yourself the most chronic and disturbing of psychiatric problems would you escape the love and the life which you are. I need to add to this list that intelligence is not a by-product of a brain better developed in you than in another. It is what you are by nature. You are knowing, you are self determining, you are self limiting, you are completely aware. But at times you may choose to suppress or to camouflage or to conceal that

Meeting *Amel*

awareness because you believe the situation in which you have placed yourself does not allow you to be fully all that you are. Or you may see that if you choose to express fully all that you are, that others in your life will not understand and accept and wish not to be involved with you anymore.

It is always what we harbor within ourselves, that darkness, fear, doubt and hesitancy which creates ALL the problems which we experience from time to time. Yet so seldom do we say "I have caused this," and as creator and sustainer, I choose to face myself and to re-create myself in harmony, in peace, in happiness, in prosperity, in lasting enjoyment and contentment.

Why is it that so many in your world, when becoming aware of this truth, decline to use it? I think if you observe them that you will find it is because they think it will take more time and energy than they believe they have to spare. Yet the maintenance of self day-by-day is no more time consuming, no more bothersome, than the brushing of your teeth or washing of your body. As each drop of rain blends together to create a puddle or a pond or a lake or an ocean, so each part of you, each thought, each feeling, each desire, is actually a part of you and blends together perfectly into one great pool of consciousness of light, of love, of life. Many of you are apprehensive to go swimming in the pool in which you are, because you believe there is some creature from the black lagoon down there waiting to snatch your body, or that someone has peed one too many times in the pool or that you might get in too deep and not come back out. It is always without any exceptions - what you are doing in yourself creates the dream or the nightmare, the pain or the pleasure, the sorrow or the happiness. The growth that you wish to experience is not something that you must wait upon until you win favor with a vengeful, fearful god as your religionists would have you to believe god to be. When you are prepared to go ahead and use and express, enjoy and share all that you have now, then god is mighty in you, powerfully revealing itself through you, and you will grow in intensity and capacity and ability to be in harmony, to be at peace, to be happy, to be prosperous, to be healthy, to be wise, to be joyful, to be loving and loved. If these things you are not prepared to make manifest in your life then please be still. . . and enjoy the space that you have created for yourself and make the most of it.

Leave others that want to take the window box of consciousness into a lush tropical rain forest. Let them do so. Do not seek to limit them by telling them it's not possible to build such a paradise in such a small window box. What they look out to see, they will create. For they are drawing from the limitless base of the inner realm - where man's mind and god's mind are one. Where man's power and god's power are one. Where man's love and god's love are one. Where man's life and god's life are one. Go now to that place within yourself and know with me the fullness of peace. Allow yourself to be totally immersed by that peace. Let each cell of your body be in harmony. Let the center within each cell radiate vitally and vibrantly the life forces which are perfectly present in it. Allow your body now. . . this very instant, to be in perfect harmony both stress and distress, fleeing that perfect peace and tranquillity. Let all disturbed emotions, and distressing thoughts, anxiety, worry and doubt and fear evaporate as a mist in the light of day. Know with me now that you are a center of consciousness, of a mind of god, powerful, penetrating all things, able to go anywhere and to do anything you choose. Know with me now that you are totally in love with yourself and with life and with all other beings. Then there can be no disharmony, no discord, no conflicts - only an ocean of good, we all draw from. Know with me now, that you are rich in all the things that you need to be creative, to be alert, to be strong, to relate one to the other in positive constructive ways. Know with me now, there is no lack, no limitation in your life. Know with me now, you are fully and completely in control of yourself and god co-creator of the cosmos. Go forth in peace, to do your perfect work. Let your light shine. Let your love radiate in the lives of all that you meet. Let your life be lived fully, joyfully and perfectly in the here and now.

Chapter 7
Communicating with the Spirit World

There is so much fear, mystery and social taboo surrounding communication with the spirit world. And I find it puzzling that so many religions forbid parishioners to engage in psychic phenomenon, seances, dream explorations or any other modes of communicating with the dead when there are so many biblical references to visions, dreams, prophets, prophesy and spirits. Religious taboo is based on fear of the unknown and this institution's need to control others by demanding ideological conformity to fearful, religious dogma.

Nevertheless, after-death experiences are not only becoming common place, they are provoking much media exposure throughout the world. This has created a receptive, non-threatening forum for others to share their experiences about communicating with their dead loved ones. There have always been people who revel in sharing or seeking ghost stories, or sightings, or poltergeist phenomenon. I was surprised and fascinated to discover that mediums have been conduits for spirits since the beginning of time. I have told you time and time again how skeptical I was about who *Seth* claimed to be, but the more I studied, the more I realized how comprehensive and credible his information is. Traveling around the country I had the opportunity to hear countless others share their experiences about apparitions of the deceased and stories about after-death experiences. Still it took several experiences where I personally explored the spiritual unknown reality to become *a believer*.

While attending classes with my physical/spiritual teacher, Carin Waddell, I discovered that it was possible to converse with entities without going into a trance. I observed in awe entire conversations between Carin and *Haré*. Some people say they hear an external voice while others, like myself, *hear* their entity speak to them telepathically. At first I thought it was me talking to myself, but during a session through Carin, *Haré* explained that what I was hearing/feeling was him periodically brushing my thoughts. That helped me become more aware of my spirit guide's assistance. I would be pondering a question when a sudden impulse would guide me to turn on the television only to find a guest on a talk show or a documentary that had the information I had internally requested. Or I would be directed to a bookshelf, select a book and find myself opening it up to the page with the relevant information. I soon realized that what I thought were merely coincidences were actually answers from *Haré*.

Eventually I began to receive a distinct feeling that my guide and the spirit guides of my students were among us during our classes. It was then that I started to fine tune and differentiate my inner voice with that of *Haré*. I only wish that my communications with my teachers could be as sophisticated as my physical/spiritual teacher, Carin. Leslie communicates with her guides and departed loved ones in sleep-state encounters. According to her guides, Leslie travels in her dreams, assisting others to heal themselves.

Communicating With The Spirit World

From time to time, Leslie and I both refer to the pendulum technique to seek answers from our inner spirits. We place our ring on a piece of thread or string and elevate it to suspend four or five inches in the air. From this still position the ring will slowly start to swing. Then we ask "yes" or "no" questions and if the ring consistently moves back and forth in a vertical move, then the answer is *yes*. However, if the ring swings in a constant horizontal line, we know our subconscious is answering *no*.

Some people use the Ouija Board as their method of communication with the spirit world. I have never had any personal success with a Ouija Board, however Leslie has had two positive experiences with the help of other partners. Many people are afraid of conjuring up evil spirits. It is my belief that you will not contact an evil spirit unless you believe you will or if you have a strong belief in evil. Fear attracts that which it fears. Although I don't believe in evil, I do believe there are ignorant and disturbed spirits who may be exposed by those humans with a similar consciousness. It is also possible to get confused or mischievous spirits on your psychic line. No matter what source you use as spirit communication, whether it is channeling, automatic writing, internal voice or any one of several other means, my advice to you is to listen objectively and use your own intuition to decide which information is beneficial to you and disregard anything that doesn't *feel* right. Refrain from listening to any spirit who demands obedience, claims to be the only truth or says you are evil. No person or entity is better than another. However, like humans, there may be some entities that are less advanced than others. Any beneficial entity will lead you to your own inner peace and wisdom and will encourage you to follow your *own* path.

Entities are not in a time frame and they can misjudge the timing of probable events. Aware spirits will preface any predictions with, *"This is only a probability because you or anyone in an event can change the course or outcome."* If you study the concept of collective consciousness, you will understand why this is true.

Sometimes entities act as mirrors and reflect back your positive beliefs and feelings. Other times they can make you feel uncomfortable if you are not being honest with yourself as they reveal your fears or erroneous beliefs. Accept that when they do this, it is out of love and a desire to help you become joyful, powerful, conscious co-creators of our own life. I have discovered that most of these teachers care little about how you feel about them. They do not require your approval, praise, thanks, validation or admonitions. Their purpose is to help you help yourself. But in the end, your life is your responsibility! Always make your decisions based on *your* feelings and never give any entity — or human being — power over you.

Our friend Gordon Stonehouse provides many other services other than trance circles with *Amel*. Besides his own psychic readings, he does karmascopes, aurascopes and will channel your spirit guide. During a channeling session with Gordon it is always interesting to listen to other people's guides to hear the different accents, personalities and syntax of delivery. For example, Leslie has an oriental guide with a soft gentle feminine voice. I feel fortunate that most of the time my guides express themselves collectively with one voice. However, we all have several guides and spirit teachers and we never know which one will come through to us in our need.

The following are two of my own guide sessions I would like to share with you.

GUIDE SESSION #1

Greetings to you. I am very pleased we finally meet in this way. You are very difficult... you are a very difficult person to capture - the attention - as many times as I have tried your attention wanders...

It is like a swarm of angry wasps descending upon decaying fruit. I am not going to be stung. I do not enjoy pain - my own or yours. Long I have tried to make myself known to you. Perhaps what I try to explain is why you've turned a deaf ear. Perhaps you've misjudged your ability and doubted what I want to do with you. You can do, and to some extent you are right to do, what I want to do with you - you must become more confident. You must have more pride in yourself. You must be more assertive!

Without knowing that you are developing, I have helped you become more self assured. You have greater esteem and respect for yourself; to be more decisive and less willing to become a plaything in the hands of those who do not value you.

To become a mighty healer helping many people, you must first know that you are well. You are strong, you are capable. If you do not know, your roots are deep in the great mother. You will fear that the winds of opposition and persecution will punch you out and leave you broken. You are learning quickly how strong you are. You have taught yourself very important lessons in very painful fashion. You have tasted of the whip! Because it has cut into your flesh - it has scarred your soul.

Everyday, I rub salt into your wounds to make you more aware of pain. Pain that exits only because you denied yourself. You doubted yourself - you hesitated to release your potential and to be the person you really are.

Now you show great promise. Now you show yourself as a serious student. Now you learn from the masters, not from fools. Soon you will not doubt. You will not hesitate to speak and to act confidently, to speak with authority, to move with the power of determination that causes people to step out of your way and let you through uninjured.

You will heal many people through transformation of their consciousness, many who will come to love you and to praise you, though many times before they have accomplished their full potential, they will curse and damn you-persecute you-heap upon you abuse. You must be strong to deal with this for not all come to greatness willingly. Many must be pushed, pulled, badgered, nagged into it! It takes great strength. Do not think that what you are developing is of little consequence. It is of much consequence. You make ready!

Guard well and carefully what you have gained in knowledge and understanding and do not return to your old ways-where sympathy and pity lead you astray, where doubt and uncertainly weakened you, where it left you disappointed. You may travel quickly, covering much ground, taking giant strides, leaping great distances, and all the while feeling like an antelope set free from captivity. FREEDOM EMPOWERS YOU TO BE YOURSELF!

Cherish the freedom you have found and build carefully upon the sure and certain knowledge of past mistakes that have revealed to you what you are not, what you cannot do, what you "should" not do. Many keys are about to be offered to you. Choose very carefully which one you keep, for it may not open to you the great treasure that you imagine behind the vault door. Use your intuition, your inner knowing, and the street smarts that you have. Do not expect GOD to shout in loud voice, for GOD my be tired and able to speak to you in a soft whisper. Whether a whisper or a shout, be ready to hear. Make yourself ready by accepting yourself- and do not reject the wisdom!

GUIDE SESSION #2

Well, you're doing it again, farting around, creating quite a noise but not a result. Waited patiently and you said that once you get material affairs in order, you would be comfortable doing spiritual work and reaching out cooperating with us again. We're waiting to see if it was a lot of gas or whether there was some substance to it.

What is it exactly that you fear? Certainly it cannot be failure, because you have failed many times and each time you managed - yes managed - to turn it around.
I must conclude that what you fear is success and the acclaim that comes with success. Surely you understand it is much harder to deal with the effect of failure than it is

to deal with the effect of success, and with success there is so much more that you can do.

In spite of all you said - of not being qualified, of never being able to have the job you really want - here you are in it. No letter after your name, no diploma hung on the wall, no mortarboard put on a shelf as a souvenir of your graduation. Proven demonstration of graduation many times over from the University of Hard Knocks. I do not recall us approving your application to become a student at the University of Hard Heads! A harder head I have never found! As hard as we knock, you refuse to open! Now realize that the only way to safeguard yourself is to write. It's the only way you will preserve self!

Surely you realize you do not need to do the actual writing. Another can use the words and connect the sentences and write the paragraphs you speak. You can give the material. She who sits by your side is more than capable of making sense of the few bits you express and can flesh out the concept. With that child -- writing -- you too may peel the onion but not in a way that causes you to shed one tear. You have had time enough on the playground - now we ring the alarm and whether you come willingly or not, you will come back into the school aware!

Times are changing and you are capable of giving birth to new seminars, workshops, concepts. We grow impatient and feel the press of those in need. We do not want the walls broken down. We want the door open wide, but in an orderly fashion, and what has been stored for safe keeping within can be dispensed and distributed. We have invaded your nights and do battle with you on the subconscious realm. We are winning! We would prefer to have your conscious cooperation and forego the need to invade your subconscious. Must not FEAR -- that if you give yourself again to this work it will take you from that which insures your material well being. We have already made certain NEVER AGAIN shall you suffer for lack of material things! We have learned our lesson well - we are committed to balance.

We'll not be swayed again by your disbelief in yourself! We'll wait no longer, both those that seek enlightenment and those that seek empowerment. And we will remind you that without any letters after your name, you have ascended a position of power. Considerable POWER! It is time for you to realize - you make a far reaching impact. You have your ego - incasing you in a suit of armor, in its very bulky form and massive weight, that will make you exceeding vulnerable and undeniably at RISK! We hand you a state of the art armor opener. Trust. Do not hesitate to free yourself. What now do you seek?

As you can tell, our spiritual teachers from the other side of life can be extremely frank, honest and often assertive. Although at times I have felt hurt and embarrased, I know their intentions are to be constructive and their guidance is given with absolute love and goodwill.

CHAPTER 8
TIME FOR A CHANGE

I will always remember my father's deathbed experience. Dad was a very proud man. Although the doctors believed he was brain dead, he nevertheless returned to his body long enough to motion with his fingers to symbolize scissors, expressing his desire to have his face shaved. The nurses standing by looked puzzled, but I knew my dad well enough to interpret the signal. They were even more confused as I stood by my father, telling him that my friends *Amel, Seth,* and *Haré* were waiting on the other side to help him with his transition. I'm sure the medical staff had occasions before to hear visitors talking to their unconscious loved ones, but I doubt if they were used to hearing guardian angels and guides called by name.

When my dad died, I knew I had reached the end of the first section of my life's play. But as I contemplated and reviewed my I.L.P. (Individual Life Plan), I realized that although I had been studying the *SETH MATERIAL* thoroughly for ten years, my outer, daily life was not flush with abundance and I was not yet living my life of total joy. I found spiritual fulfillment reading and teaching the *SETH MATERIAL,* and my interaction with nature provided serenity. But it was still apparent to me that I enjoyed the feeling that alcohol provided. I think one of my attractions to beer and music was the ability it gave me to go within and actually live in the *now*. It would still be another five years of pushing events before I would learn to enjoy music, life and living in the now without alcohol.

But the major area in my life where I was still deficient was in the area of prosperity. My financial situation failed to reflect my teaching beliefs. As a medical aide supervisor and part time transportation coordinator, I only made $7,000.00 a year. Although my job was fun, I was ready for abundance and new opportunities. Fortunately I had my summers off, which gave me the freedom to fly around the country conducting driver training workshops. Then, in the summer of 1980, I conducted an extensive workshop to train all the school bus drivers who transported students with disabilities in the state of Louisiana. It was a large undertaking, but very rewarding. At the end of the session, many of the drivers came up to thank me and assure me that the information I provided would really help them. I knew the importance of training. After all, by this time I'd been a teacher/trainer for some years. But something in the way they expressed their gratitude suddenly made me realize what a *really* valuable service I was offering. This was my first real lesson in understanding the concept of how much you deserve for your services. I raised my fee from $100.00 a workshop to $250.00. School districts didn't seem to mind paying me that daily fee, and, of course, I wish I had asked for this amount sooner.

Throughout this period, my relationship with Leslie had intensified and although I was seeing other women, and even traveling with them, Leslie continued her unwavering loyalty. Leslie was also ready for a change in her life and after much discussion, we decided to move to Florida together. We agreed that I should go down for a few days first to plant seeds for classes and workshops based on the *SETH MATERIAL.* During a trance circle with *Amel,* he suggested that I make every effort to learn proper social etiquette in order to *"know what to do with that extra fork at the table."* This was his way of preparing me for the wealthy and culturally refined people that would be attracted to my seminars and classes. All of the participants at the trance circle also got a laugh when *Amel* recommended that I park my old rusty, beat up 1970 Impala several blocks away from people's homes or seminar locations! Little did I know at that time how right and how valuable *Amel's* advice would be.

Before Leslie and I moved to Florida, we decided to move in together in order to save up some money. Soon after her divorce, my friend Sally had moved to Florida. She still had a beautiful home back in Ohio, with a lovely yard full of trees and she offered to let us live there rent free in exchange for taking care of the house while she had it on the market to sell. This was a fantastic opportunity for us because not only were we living rent-free, but it definitely enhanced our prosperity consciousness! This home was decorated with beautiful furnishings that exuded quality and prosperity. And best of all, the house had a fireplace. Leslie and I love fireplaces! This experience was the catalyst for other prosperity lessons that helped us recognize other abundance opportunities.

I will never forget saying good bye to my mom. She cried and I knew she was having as much difficulty letting me go as I was leaving her. Nevertheless I was anxious and enthusiastic about creating a new reality that would be consistent with my *Seth* beliefs. Sometimes merely the decision to take a risk and conclude a chapter in your life will set the scene for new manifestations. Leslie and I left for Florida...it was time for new beginnings!

❖ ❖ The Florida Experience ❖ ❖

Leslie and I were not sure where we really wanted to settle in Florida, so we took my spirit teacher's advice and decided to be spontaneous. First we explored the west coast of Forida but we finally settled in south Florida. It had it's advantages. I had conducted some *Seth* seminars there the previous fall and I still had some contacts there. And our friend Sally lived close by in Boynton Beach.

What an area. The sights we saw on our first drive around opulent Palm Beach were incredible. I have never seen so many Rolls Royces, Mercedes and Excallibers in the same place!. We were in awe of the magnificent mansions with their sculptured bushes and detailed landscaping. Of course, at the time, we couldn't afford Palm Beach, so we found a suitable apartment in Fort Lauderdale, but we spent many Sunday afternoons driving through this wonderland. Palm Beach represented to us the epitome of opulence and prosperity. What a way to enhance and develop our prosperity consciousness!

Initially Leslie and I talked about getting separate apartments since independence was important to both of us. But although I had seminars scheduled, I really didn't have any individual students or any money coming in on a regular basis and Leslie had to start her search for a job, so we decided to share an apartment. Little did we know — or were even ready to accept — at the time that we would still be "significant others" many years later.

Our Florida experience exceeded all of my expectations. My dream of working for myself came to fruition, with all of the obvious challenges of self-employment. I learned two important elements during my time in Florida: I learned how to attract abundance and enhanced my teaching/intuition skills. I can't tell you how many times I thought we would be unable to make our rent or car payment when suddenly a school district would call wanting a workshop or a student would request an individual session or intuitive counseling. Often, the amount of money I earned from those last minute requests would be exactly the amount needed to pay a bill. I was learning that situations other people would assume were not connected or were merely coincidental, were actually examples of how the laws of manifestation can work for us if only we would allow it.

Initially I placed ads in local papers offering seminars based on the *SETH MATERIAL*. After the workshop, I would offer participants an opportunity to attend weekly classes. After attending weekly classes, members were invited to come to our on-going *Seth* class. This class met every week from 1984 until Leslie and I moved to California in 1986. I only wish I could include all the names of the many friends we made during our time in Florida. There were those who remained in our group the entire time while others came and went whenever they needed inspiration or stimulation or just to spend some time with like-minded souls. Most of the people we met were grateful to discover other people who believed in reincarnation and the theory that we create our own reality. For years they longed to know others who not only shared their philosophies, but who lived them. I was fortunate to have Leslie and my mom who share my philosophies, but many of my students were reluctant to share these ideas with family, friends and coworkers. So our sessions became not only a place for learning consciousness raising, but also a family environment.

We invited our friend Gordon down from Ohio to conduct trance circles with *Amel.* Gordon was so successful he started to come on a regular basis. He helped many of my students on their road to consciously creating their own reality, and his popularity attracted many other people to my seminars, classes and individual sessions. We had the privilege and pleasure of working with hundreds of people in Florida. My experiences from those days are among some of my favorite memories.

I think Leslie might have enjoyed this time better if she didn't have to work a typical 9-to-5 job. Self-employment provided me with a flexible schedule so I could also continue to conduct workshops nationwide to train bus drivers. Periodically, I worked as a substitute vocational instructor at a Fort Lauderdale ARC sheltered workshop for persons with developmental disabilities. This was very convenient, because I could work there when I wasn't flying around the country doing workshops or during times when my local classes and seminars were slow. I experienced another of those *co-incidences* while working at this agency.

Whenever I would substitute, I would go to lunch with Ginnie Miller, one of the other teachers. After several lunches, Ginnie wanted to know what I did when I wasn't filling in for someone at the workshop. I'm usually reluctant to give specifics about my *Seth* work to someone I don't know well, so I gave her a general statement about offering sessions on how to create your own reality. Ginnie responded, *"Have you ever heard of the* SETH MATERIAL*?"* I believe for as long as I live, I will forever be fascinated by the way the manifestations of our inner life continue to affect our outer life. Ginnie went on to tell me about meeting a man who interviewed Robert Rutts and Jane Roberts in a video production that included a *Seth* session. I was very excited and wanted to know where I could get a copy of this tape, but Ginnie didn't know. Nevertheless, I knew that this tape would appear sooner or later. If my intent, faith and desire was intense nothing could prevent me from drawing in that tape. Several years later I was contacted by Richie Kendall, a former member of the original Jane Roberts/*Seth* class, who happened to be one of the people responsible for the production of this tape and who was in the process of marketing them. Not only did I get a copy of the tape, but Richie and I collaborated together on a *Seth* workshop in Florida.

I only wish I had the time and space to write about all of the success stories I had the opportunity to witness during my time in Florida. In fact much of the material I used to write *BELIEFOLOGY: RAISING YOUR CONSCIOUSNESS TO WEALTH, HEALTH, AND HAPPINESS* came from my experiences there. It was during this period of time that I developed a personal belief profile that I used in individual sessions with students which later became the basis for the *BELIEFOLOGY WORKBOOK*. Most of my students were women. Many of them were divorced or wanted to leave their partners, but financial fears were preventing them from terminating their relationship. This was especially difficult for those women who sacrificed their education or careers in order to raise their children while their husbands became extremely successful in business. After lots of belief work which enhanced self-esteem, some of these students terminated their marriages and even went on to establish themselves in business. This gave me the idea for creating a workshop called *Discovering Your Life's Purpose and Attracting Abundance*.

One of my students from this class became a very successful design artist and another designed and created her own line of women's and children's clothes that were displayed on a segment of *Good Morning America*. One of my students, Billie Petty, became my public relations agent. She had experience promoting psychics and she had contacts through her ex-husband, a television producer who was instrumental in giving Sally Jessie Raphael an opportunity early in her career. Billie got me spots on radio talk shows and helped coordinate several seminars. The most memorable one was conducted at the Fontainbleau Hotel, in Miami Beach. It was at this seminar that I met our friends Marty and Joanie Segal. During the introduction of all of my *Seth* seminars I always ask each participant to share how they discovered the *SETH MATERIAL* and how they found out about my seminar. Many of the stories focused on a *co-incidence*. One lady recalled how a *Seth* book fell off the shelf at the library and literally hit her in the head during a time when her life was in shambles. Another participant told the story of how she had meant to throw away her newspaper several times, but never got around to it. Finally, on the way outside to take the paper to the dumpster, she glanced down and saw my seminar ad in the classified. She was so grateful because she had yearned to discuss this material with someone for years. Marty and Joanie had also wanted to meet other people to share metaphysical "stuff". They rarely read the classified ads but on this one day they found my ad and discovered I was offering my *Seth* seminar right down the street from their penthouse. Marty is a trial attorney who later helped me incorporate my first company, Individual Growth and Fulfillment (I.G.F.). Instead of starting a center or some sort of esoteric church, I preferred to create a school without walls that could include the services of people like Gordon and others who were teaching metaphysics. Marty eventually wrote a book *THE GURU IS YOU,* that included

Time For A Change

some of our experiences as well as his reaction to the *Amel* sessions.

After a string of successful seminars, Billie and I decided to offer another workshop in the Miami area. I spent more money than ever to market the seminar, but only four people signed up. *Amel* often told me, *"Success doesn't equate to the number of students but what you can share with those who attend and you never know the seeds you may plant with those you assist."* This was certainly true in the case of Chuck and Lynn Lockwood who were two of the participants at that seminar. Leslie and I count the Lockwood's among the best friends we made in Florida. They lived in Coconut Grove in an exceptionally beautiful and unique glass house. Lynn was a talented decorator with exquisite taste. The master bedroom opened onto a balcony overlooking the swimming pool and the family room, with it's view of nature, was conducive to holding our trance circles. Throughout the years, our relationship with the Lockwood's has proved to be a reciprocal prosperity lesson. Not only did a good friendship evolve, but we have each gained some mutual financial benefits from our meeting at that seminar.

So *Amel* was right when he predicted we would be interacting with rich, elegant and refined people. I remember being in awe of the ocean view and the tasteful furniture of an actor's home in Palm Beach County where Gordon/*Amel* held a session for his guests. I loved giving private sessions for students at their pool side. I even held sessions each week for one student at her home beside her *indoor* pool. I learned a lot about money from these people. Some people had no difficulty attracting money but they had a problem keeping it. Others might as well not have had their money because they were so fearful of *losing* it that it prevented them from *enjoying* it. And I learned that the answer to the age-old question of *"how much money is enough"* is relative. What is a lot for some people is viewed as poverty by others!

Florida provided me with a good life. Students from my class would invite Leslie and I to spend the day on their yacht. I even had one student fly us to the Bahamas for my birthday on his private plane. I've always wanted the freedom to experience as much of life as I could and to live in opulent, comfortable environments and experiences like this made me yearn for more. I guess you could say I started to get greedy. I began to wonder . . . If I can attract this fulfillment in Florida, surely with the abundance in California I could be even more successful.

❖ ❖ California Dreaming ❖ ❖

Ever since the sixties I've always wanted to live in California. I guess I thought it would all be like Haight-Ashberry and the hippie scene of 1967. And it didn't take much to encourage Leslie to move, because she lived in California in 1973 and also had California fever. Although in the early days of conversing with spirits, I would ask for guidance on even the most mundane decisions, for the most part, I've always been very stubborn and definitely an independent thinker. This was certainly evident when we embarked upon our California dream even though on several occasions *Amel* emphatically stated that this move was neither appropriate nor well timed. We packed everything we could into our two cars and sold or gave away all our other furniture and household possessions. We decided to follow *Seth's* advice from THE NATURE OF

Time For A Change

INDIVIDUAL AND MASS EVENTS and just follow our impulses. I had conducted *Seth* workshops for people in the LA area so we decided to head in that direction.

When we arrived we knew we would have to find jobs until I could get my seminars and classes started. There were two jobs advertised in the *LA TIMES* that were live-in positions for group homes: one up north in Petaluma and the other in the San Fernando Valley. We ended up taking the job in Sepulveda in the San Fernando Valley where we lived with six men who had developmental disabilities. I was extremely concerned about Leslie's ability to live with eight people because she prefers to keep to herself. Much to my surprise, she acclimated better than I did. Initially, this was an ideal arrangement, because while the guys went to a daytime workshop, Leslie worked as a medical assistant and I could travel around the country doing workshops and consulting. We were paid very little cash since the agency provided room and board, so this added income was a plus.

We discovered that living in California was expensive. What a shock I had when I went to get a license tag for our new car! I laughed at the LA county clerk when she asked for an amount that was equivalent to two car payments. I actually thought she was joking! And the traffic was unbelievable. Sometimes it seemed like my drive from LAX (Los Angeles airport) to our home in the Valley seemed further than my plane trips. But my biggest disappointment was the competition from other spiritual and self-improvement practitioners. It seemed as though there was a channeler or some sort of a psychic on every block.

Every other weekend we had respite coverage at the group home that gave us a chance to get away and explore other areas of California. We fell in love with the San Diego area and made plans to move there. Although I was attracting some interesting students to my classes, because of the competition, I wasn't drawing the number of students I needed to even pay for all the advertising and promotional materials. It became obvious that I was going to have to find a job, at least temporarily, that would give me a pay check on a regular basis. Within a few weeks, I found a job in the San Diego area managing an Intermediate Care Facility (I.C.F.) for persons with severe developmental disabilities.

It was a tearful, emotional good-bye when Leslie and I left the group home. We would miss the residents as much as they were going to miss us. The parents of some of the men even offered to pay us out of their own pocket to keep us in LA. But we were determined to make the move.

Like LA, San Diego was also very expensive and now we were responsible for our own rent and food as well as the daily living expenses. Soon it became evident that *Amel* was correct — the timing just wasn't right for our move to California. By this time Leslie and I were deep into credit card debt, using new credit cards to pay off old ones. Finally I filed for bankruptcy, but even with this relief, we still struggled to pay our daily living expenses. My salary from the human services agency combined with Leslie's earnings from her job was not enough to get ahead of the bills. I had helped so many people in the past to understand that it is essential not to get stuck in the moment, but I couldn't help feeling that things looked pretty hopeless for us. Then our friends Chuck and Lynn Lockwood heard about our financial situation and mailed us a check for $3,000.00. Words can never express our gratitude. At first Leslie and I were extremely reluctant and too proud to accept the check. But, as things happen, we came upon a book about prosperity that emphasized the importance of learning how to receive. We did accept the money and not only did it provide temporary security, it revealed to us once

Time For A Change

again that the universe supports us when we need it. We knew we were truly blessed with good friends.

For the next few months, I tried to create the same interest in my classes and workshops I'd experienced in Florida, but all my efforts failed. It was time to make a decision. We considered returning to Florida but although Florida had been good to us, Leslie and I decided to move back to Ohio. Once again the universe responded. Our friend Sally still needed someone to care for her house in Fairborn, Ohio, and so Leslie and I returned to the same beautiful home that we had left four years ago. We had come full circle. The house exuding quality and grace that was the catalyst that prepared our prosperity consciousness for our move to Florida, would now serve as a safe haven to prepare us for the next chapter in our life together.

CHAPTER 9
COMING HOME

Initially, I felt that bankruptcy and my inability to get established in California represented a failure on my part. It took some serious introspection to recognize the importance of examining the big picture. But *"in the moment"* it was hard to put my faith in the belief that what appeared to be a negative event or experience was sowing the seeds for new, positive growth with unlimited potential. Leslie returned to her old job at the laboratory where she had worked before we moved to Florida. I wasn't sure what to do. I knew my passion and purpose in this life was to teach self-improvement and metaphysics, but I also knew that practicality called for getting a temporary job. Doing what?

Nevertheless, it was good to be back home and close to family again. I was pleased to see that my mom had developed a very healthy relationship with a gentleman named Walt. She was healthy and enjoying life, traveling and interested in sharing her new experiences with us. And Leslie's parents lived close enough so we could do things with them, too.

One day Leslie saw an article in the newspaper about a progressive social services agency called Choices in Community Living. This agency provided residential services to persons with developmental disabilities. I applied for a job and although I had experience in the field, I didn't have a degree, so I had to start as a direct care worker making $5.00 per hour. Then one evening at an agency social event, I had a chance to talk to my boss, Tom Weaver, about my past experience in the area of disabilities, including my consulting throughout the country. Soon afterwards, Choices came to me with an interesting offer. They put me on contract to help *"grow"* the agency in different directions. This was definitely a win-win situation because I was able to help Choices grow as well as create a permanent job for myself as Foster Care and Semi Independent Living Coordinator.

Once again I drew in the ideal job — helping people help themselves — a job supervising people that allowed me to be creative. There was just one problem. My position came with significant responsibilities. However, since I didn't have a degree my pay was different from those people with a degree. It was time to go back to my own personal belief profile and examine my beliefs in the area of career and prosperity.

Overall, I spent three very fulfilling years with Choices, but I knew it was time to resume my spiritual work. Leslie and I both started to get traveling and adventure fever but we were still trying to get through our financial difficulties. About that time, both Carin Waddell and my friend Ginny in Fort Lauderdale, recommended a book entitled *CREATING MONEY* by Sanaya Roman and Duane Packer that was channeled by their spirit guides, *Orin* and *Daben*. With the insights from this book, in tandem with the exercise I'd developed and utilized with my students throughout the years, I made more progress in six months on my prosperity consciousness then in all my other years of work put together. I finally overcame the major erroneous belief that I needed a degree to make the money I deserved.

I've always attracted jobs with purpose and responsibilities so I obviously had that positive belief. Now I was ready to test the newest part of my belief system. I sent out resumes and received a call from Dr. Valerius, with the Butler County Board of Mental Retardation and Developmental Disabilities. Because of my experience, especially in the area of developing supported living arrangements for people who historically lived in institutions, I was hired as a Developer of Community Options. The superintendent, Lloyd Harris, was a visionary and was willing to pay me as much as a person with a degree. Leslie and I moved to Fairfield, Ohio with the idea that we would stay about two years before moving back to either the ocean or the mountains. Little did we know that my career would keep me in Ohio for another decade.

My new prosperity consciousness was working. My new position was with the government, so I didn't have the flexibility to take days off for my bus driver consulting work. I had to use vacation days as I accrued them and I decided to raise my workshop fees to compensate. But the school districts I contacted didn't seem to have a problem with my new rates and I started to get calls.

CREATING MONEY definitely helped me attract abundance and opportunities. Although I always considered the *SETH MATERIAL* and the written dictation from *Haré* to provide comprehensive information about manifesting the life you want, these new spirit teachers *Orin* and *Daben* along with continued assistance from *Amel* proved to be the most helpful to me in regard to *material manifestation*. Several years later I began to correspond with a spirit guide, *Teach,* who would assist with health issues. It has become evident to me that there are many different spiritual entities because each one has a different approach and can offer you different experiences at different times in your life.

I'd been working for the County Board a year when I heard about a social services agency called Residential Alternatives for individuals with Developmental Disabilities, that was interviewing for an Executive Director and CEO position. Usually positions of this type require a minimum of a bachelors degree and most agencies require a masters degree. But I applied anyway, and to my delight I was hired. I had finally succeeded in eliminating the belief that I had to have a degree to do what I wanted and to be paid well for it. Through my leadership, RADD has grown from one employee to 80 employees and increased it's revenue from $35,000 a year to a million and a half. My next book, *HUMAN SERVICES IN THE NEW MILLENNIUM*, will describe my experiences in the area of human services and home care.

RADD provided me with lots of challenges and growth opportunities as well as the freedom to continue my consulting. In 1993, I received a call from Denise Lasley, Vice President of AMS Distributors, Inc., a Georgia company that produces and distributes video training programs. AMS was interested in developing a series of training video programs based on my workshop for school bus drivers transporting students with disabilities. It was a wonderful opportunity for me and I agreed. But during the period Denise and her husband Del (President of AMS) brought their production crew to Ohio to film my work, my personal life was full of stress. My sister, suffering from her twenty-year heroin addiction, had spent time in and out of nursing homes through the years. She had just come out of a coma and was insisting on leaving the hospital although she was going to be homeless. Furthermore, on the front page of that Sunday's *DAYTON DAILY NEWS*, there was

Coming Home

an article about my sister and her career as a prostitute along with other things about my family that I never knew. This article had my mother extremely agitated and I had to keep her calm while trying to deal with the overall situation. Nevertheless, as they say in show business *"the show must go on"*, so Leslie and I took Del and Denise out to dinner one evening to discuss the progress of the video production. Although in the course of conversation nothing was mentioned about metaphysics, when we returned home Leslie expressed to me her strong intuitive feeling that both Del and Denise would be very much involved in the future of our spiritual mission.

Several weeks later, Leslie's father, Karl, 67, a man who was rarely sick, returned home from work and told his wife Martha that he was going to lie down for a while because he wasn't feeling well. Ten minutes later Leslie's mom went to check on him and he was dead. I truly feel that if we listen to the messages from our *internal life* it will often reveal the future to our *external life*. Just two days before, on Thanksgiving evening as we were leaving Leslie's parent's house, Karl, who would always engage me in a hearty handshake, grabbed my hand and instead brought me to him with a compassionate hug. I'm a hugger by nature and in the past when I tried to hug Karl, he would put up some resistance. That night I think Karl knew subconsciously that he would be dying two days later and the hug was his way of saying good-bye and take good care of his daughter. *(See* Teach's *dictation.)*

My sister Cherie died the following spring. I can't begin to try and describe my sister for it would take a book to properly illustrate her unique personality. But I believe that if she had been compelled to work on her self-esteem, she would have accomplished more than I can ever imagine. She was full of energy, creativity, passion, enthusiasm and intellectual potential. Her greatest gift to the world was her daughter Paula, who has decided to make better choices than her mother. Paula went on to graduate from college and has entered the rehabilitation field to help others help themselves.

The video production seemed to be the silver lining during this tragic time. My first royalty check from AMS motivated me to finally do what my spiritual teachers had suggested I do for years — write! Leslie and I used that first check to take a first-class trip to New York City: hotels, restaurants, cabs and all. But what was so different about this trip was we paid cash for everything. It allowed us the freedom from worry so we could spend time imagining the future.

Although our outer life often provides us with hints of previews of things to come, it is our internal utterances that reveal the preferred outcomes. Leslie was correct; the Lasley's would be involved in our spiritual endeavors. The National Safety Council asked me to do a presentation in San Diego and guess who I ran into there — the Lasley's. It was no coincidence. We met one evening in the hotel's lounge and during the conversation Denise and I discovered that we were both interested in reincarnation as well as other esoteric philosophies. I told her about an idea for a book I wanted to write. I learned that in addition to being an experienced video editor, Denise is also a print editor and she expressed an interest in helping me edit and publish my book. After the trip, we began the awkward process of working together on the project long distance. Thank goodness for an 800 number, because we logged many hours preparing my first book *BELIEFOLOGY* for publication.

Several months later, when Denise and I really needed to meet to discuss the finishing touches for the book, we discovered that we were both scheduled to be in New Orleans at the same time for different seminars. Isn't synchronicity fascinating. I can't type, so my friends Merrianne and Michelle typed my manuscript. Leslie and Denise helped me co-write and design the book. And Del is assisting in the marketing. Once again life supports us with whatever we need.

Take some time now to examine your life in retrospect and see how your past may be full of what seemed like coincidences, but were really events and relationships you created to synchronize future, fulfilling events. How about the times you gave freely of your time, resources or money, sometimes receiving back in kind from the original source or from an unexpected source or opportunity? Remember our friends Chuck and Lynn who helped us out of our financial difficulties without being asked? Ten years later they ran into financial challenges and I had the opportunity to help them. Ironically enough it was almost 10 years to the date that they had so generously helped us.

The winds of change are definitely blowing through the nineties. Every sentient being receives intense impulses from their internal soul, yearning to become free of former painful patterns of living. The more erroneous beliefs we uncover and replace with positive ones the more we will come to understand our true selves and our true relationship with father/mother God.

CHAPTER 10
TEACH: EXPLORING MY BELIEFS/CONSCIOUSNESS

As I grew, I continued to become more aware, and began to lovingly release my self-limiting beliefs. Yet I often wondered why I continued to attract some of my health challenges when it seemed that others with more negative attitudes stayed so healthy. Finally, I have learned to take the advice I give to my students. I stress that you can not compare your progress with that of others because we each have different erroneous beliefs from our past that we are working on eliminating, along with self-limiting beliefs from future life times that are happening simultaneously. In addition, comparing is judgmental, and in order to heal and gain the growth and freedom you aspire to, it is imperative not to judge yourself, but simply to love and accept yourself just as you are now. When you do this, you will naturally evolve from choice versus compulsion or fear. At first, I had more fears because of my vulnerability as I learned to expose my undesirable beliefs, responses and actions in preparation to releasing them. Many people experience this same reaction. Others, especially *"victims"* prefer to rationalize their beliefs and play it safe with their choices and awareness thus delaying any major growth.

Nevertheless, eventually *the self* seeks freedom. This become very apparent to me when I finally decided to self expose my fears about death. Though I thought I had worked through my fears of death, I discovered that I still had some concerns. This became evident to me during a trip Leslie and I took one year to the upper peninsula of Michigan, where we often go to enjoy some time in the clean air and to absorb the beauty of the lakes and the birch trees. One evening, we decided to go the local Indian reservations casino. After a while, we went our separate ways to gamble on various slot machines, with the understanding that we would look for each other in about an hour. Because the casino was packed with people and filled with all of the usual loud sounds of slot machines, bells going off and the typical excitement of the crowd, it was extremely difficult to find Leslie. The casino was divided into at least three major rooms and I think what happened is that just about the time I would leave one room looking for Leslie she probably entered it. We must have spent at least an hour searching for each other. During the search, I began to wonder if death was like this. Are there those individuals who wander aimlessly looking for a familiar face? When we finally found each other, I immediately shared my new found thoughts and fears about death with Leslie.

Ironically, when we arrived back at our hotel and turned on the television we heard about Princess Diana's fatal accident. This led to an intense discussion about why Diana and the others chose to die in that crash. According to the beliefs that I subscribe to, that *like consciousness attracts like consciousness,* you can attract negative events to you like illness, accidents and detrimental relationships, as well as positive events. We usually don't choose death on a conscious level, but the inner-self, along with the oversoul, always chooses the time, place and type of death. Once you realize and accept this you will not only perceive future deaths differently but you will find it interesting to explore the possibilities and/or causes of the death of people from history. Would Lincoln or Kennedy be as popular had they not been assassinated? Could Martin Luther King have accomplished more in his pursuit of racial equality or was his truly a timely death? These questions have been asked many times. What are the answers?

Every person killed in any accident — in a plane crash, in a natural catastrophe, in a car crash or an explosion — has, on some level, acquiesced to the outcome. Wouldn't it be fascinating to know the particular situation of each passenger on the Titanic to discover the reason or purpose why some survived and so many others died. There were not enough life boats on board, that's the official, and obvious reason. But what were the underlying reasons? Remember, your life is like a play where you are the director, casting the characters and creating the events that define your life *and death*.

When a former student from Florida, Billie Petty, moved to Texas, she was fortunate to meet Jeff King who channels an entity who refers to himself *as Teach*. Although Jeff orally channels *Teach*, Jeff periodically takes written dictation too and he agreed to help me with some questions. There were some things I wanted to know. Many people claim they are not fearful of death, but how many of those individuals believe that when they die they join their departed loved ones for an eternal retirement? In addition, I was in a quandary on whether or not to title this book *INTERNAL LIFE: I DO BELIEVE IN SPIRIT* or use the plural *SPIRITS*. Here are my questions and *Teach's* responses:

Questions:

1. I'm currently working on my new book *INTERNAL LIFE: I DO BELIEVE IN SPIRITS*. Would it be more appropriate to say *SPIRIT* (singular) or *SPIRITS* (plural)?

Jeff gave me permission last year to use any of our written sessions in this publication. I'm hoping that some of the insights that you assisted me in, especially health issues, will enable others to heal themselves and allow life to unfold naturally. In addition, I have Gordon's permission to use *Amel* material and most of the book will be my personal journal on how I've consciously become aware of the internal life in all external manifestations. I want to include information about death. When I was doing my belief work, what I thought was a severe fear of death turned out to be more of a reluctance to give up all the things/people on earth. The thought of not experiencing a thunderstorm, an ocean, and woods and not being a part of another spring time/tulips really scared me. In addition, I'm sure my strong ego played a part in this fear.

I think I've overcome this fear because if we do create our reality just like our dreams, after death we would be able to create spring or earth-like conditions through our psyche. Right?? The other reality that I've come to terms with is the loss of loved ones. I realize, unlike most Christians, that there isn't a heaven where you meet your friends and relatives. I know that in death, like life, the departed have a choice if they want to see you upon your transition. As I stated in *BELIEFOLOGY* — *"there is a good-bye to every relationship"* and this acceptance has enabled me to appreciate and enjoy relationships — not taking my relationships for granted, being in the moment with people like my mom and Leslie, living in the moment. The other _major_ fear I had was after reading those philosophies that stated that after a transition period after death that you would lose your conscious identity and merge into the whole. We have discussed this before and I choose to believe instead that all life/time is simultaneous and that no identity is ever lost. If this is so, how would *Amel* or *Seth* recall/remember or be conscious of their "past" life times?

Please comment on the aforementioned and make any remarks on the topic of internal life in general that you and Jeff would feel comfortable with.

2. Leslie started a new job that she hates — any suggestions?

3. When I was born, due to a complicated pregnancy the doctor thought I would be born mentally retarded. Obviously, although I work with individuals with disabilities I'm not retarded. However, I did have several learning disabilities requiring speech therapy until I was in the sixth grade. Lately (last several years) on certain days it's very difficult for me to express myself verbally. I'm starting to see a correlation with nights when I didn't keep my C-pap mask on for the sleep apnea. Is this language/concentration/alertness related to a lack of oxygen to the brain? Or my learning disability? I think I've resolved the origin/causation of the sleep apnea and with a planned weight loss I will resolve the apnea. Why did I co-create the difficult pregnancy and speech problems?

TEACH'S ANSWER:

My Dear Ken,

On the issue of death, there are many, many difficulties in discussing the after-physical-life environment in ways that are similar to discussing simultaneous time. The physical life focus makes certain things seem "for granted," and it is difficult to discard that filter when thinking about the issue, even in one's own private thoughts.

What that means is that this discussion will make liberal use of analogy, metaphor, stories, parables, etc., as ways to at least look around the filter if not discarding it.

First, the after-physical-life environment is just as much a creation of one's own doing as is the physical environment of the just-completed life. The big difference, of course, is that there is no time lag between intent and experience. Without that time lag, the being inhabiting such an environment is often "momentarily" befuddled. Imagine what would happen to you if every one of your thoughts became instantly physical in this reality! Such an experience in corporeal existence would lead any physical human quickly to insanity.

What occurs, though, with a recently deceased individuation (my work for the individual whose conscious has been associated with a physical body for X number of years in physical reality) is that the adjustment is made through a sort of "coming home" process. In the grand scheme of things, 70, or 90, or 120 physical years as a physical lifetime is inconsequential as a time frame within the infinity of time.

That individuation is most certainly not inconsequential in terms of impact and contribution to the overall process of contributing to being-ness, however. One of the things that recently physically-orientated individuations grapple with upon physical death, is an attempt to hold on to the focus of the just completed physical life. That physical life focus no longer serves in the new environment, so it must be discarded. Attempting to cling stubbornly to the focus is what sometimes causes the phenomenon in physical reality often described as "ghosts".

Now, you have discussed your fear of death, some of the reasons for it, and a bit about how you have resolved this issue consciously. It is true, for example, that someone who clings to the physical focus as the baseline of experience will have difficulty adjusting in the "afterlife" (I dislike that term, but it serves as a matter of convenience here). If that person is someone who cherishes corporeal existence for the sensual pleasures of the existence – sights, sounds, experiences, etc. – then such a focus may become the baseline against which reality is measured. It will be difficult to make sense of the afterlife reality in the absence of externally provided stimuli.

It will not, however, be difficult to make the adjustment as soon as the individuation realizes that the creation of all external stimuli, in the new non-physical environment, occurs from within. Some hard-liners might say this is "playing God"; that is, suggesting that the individuation can create external stimuli only with thought. Well, I say that is exactly the point! The truth about reality and about all beings' places in reality is that they participate as creators, that it is their responsibility to be excellent creators, that they fulfill themselves by being creators, and that because all of this is true, they should exalt in their ability to create the reality they inhabit.

Religions usually frown upon such concepts, but they are very empowering ideas.

You have made peace with yourself on the issue by consciously accepting the fact that you will be able to create the sunsets that you previously believed would have been so difficult to "live without" in your new environment. And so you shall.

Further, it is also possible to create any literal, physical environment and inhabit it physically if you so desire in order to remind yourself of the sensual nature of physical existence. You are correct, therefore, in feeling "relieved" that you will not have to give up any of your goodies in order to become a non-physical being.

The more common fear of death, though, is a fear arising from not knowing what is on the other side. The conjecture about what is on the other side - whether it is the other side of the River Styx, the other side of the Great Mountain, or the other side of heaven - has occupied humankind for millennia. Because no one has been there and come back to report on the experience, at least in a way that your scientists and researchers could verify in physical reality, there has been no way for people with this kind of fear of death to overcome their fear.

People who have had "death experiences" and then been revived, as on the operating table, often report certain experiences during the time of their clinical deaths. These are untrustworthy recounts because they are descriptions filtered through physical senses. The individuals must use physical tools to describe the experience (meaning, physical *mouths, tongues, etc., and put the experience into physical words), so they can not convey the reality of the situation as it truly exists. The descriptions they provide are metaphors.*

It is not coincidental that so often these metaphors are similar. That is to be expected. You would expect to hear similar descriptions of an event from people who grew up in the same neighborhood, had the same values, and were physically similar in their sensing apparatus (eyes, ears, nose, etc.). Well, compared to the vast differentiation's that exists in the true breadth of reality, the human viewpoint is a viewpoint from "the same neighborhood by a group of folks with the same ideas who look pretty muck alike."

Take any non-physical experience that possesses the expansiveness of unbridled, unencumbered reality and have a human describe it, and you will have a description that will be quite similar to another human's description of it. Should two dogs describe it, their descriptions would be similar, though they would be quite different from the humans'.

You get the point.

So, the metaphor I will use is that "immediately" after physical death there is a transition to a large, wonderful theater where the dearly departed can create his own play. Some folks decide to re-create their physical lives as fully as they can in order to build a "safe place" in which to reorient themselves. Other people start running around the theater, joyfully looking under every seat to try to discover ways to play in their new surroundings. Other individuals look for the controls for the lights, the microphones, etc., and immediately start trying to shape their environment more precisely to their liking.

Other actors appear on the stage as needed. Spooks such as I happen along from "time to time" in order to assume roles that will help these newly re-integrating individuals understand their new home without fearing for their safety or their sanity.

This, incidentally, is the reason why the death experiences of operating room patients often include comments about deceased friends and relatives showing up "at the end of the tunnel." It could be a fragment of that previously dead (physically) individuation, but it is often an actor meant to help in the transition process.

Is this "pulling a trick" on the dying person? Most certainly not! It is a learning experience meant to, among other reasons, help explain that manifestation in the new environment goes by a vastly more expansive set of rules than the manifestation "rule" of the environment that is being left behind.

Very quickly, though, discussions like the paragraph above become moot. When the truth about non-physical reality is realized, then there is no need for a "guide." The ability to learn is unlimited, and the just-deceased individual jumps into that process with both feet.

Does the individuation that has just ceased physical existence ever lose the "memory" of that existence? It is not lost in any irretrievable manner. It can be filed away, and the file drawer may not be opened if that is the choice of the individuation, but the memory exists forever and is accessible to all – not just to the individuation.

In the non-judgmental reality that is non-physical existence, such a thing is not seen as an "invasion of *privacy" because All That Is is all that is. In a true understanding of being-ness, any entity can observe the peccadilloes of any other entity without judgment and with loving regard. Therefore, the life of Ken Routson, physical human in the 20th century, will never be lost. It will always be available as a source of learning and source of comfort for whomever wishes to gaze upon it. Yes, even in spirit of any and all "dirty little secrets" swept under the rug of consciousness during physical reality. The entire life of Ken Routson, and any other being, is a tableaux for appreciation by All That Is, so there will never be any point at which that life will not be available for perusal.*

This is the reason non-physical beings can recall "past lives" (whether those lives are in the past or the future as humans think of the terms). It is the reason that you, right now, have available to you the memories of all of your parallel, probable, future, and past lives.

Relationships in physical life can "carry over" into non-physical life, but that is rare. The reason for the rarity is that such connections are usually dealt with over multiple physical lifetimes if there is benefit to multiple interactions for the purpose of addressing life issues. In non-physical reality, "relationships" are created instantaneously if such a relationship serves a learning purpose.

As to re-integration into All That Is: it will happen. That does not mean, however, that any being will ever lose one whit of individuality. There are individual drops within the largest ocean, and both exist as part of the other. Being part of a whole is sublime, but that does not mean the forfeit of individuality.

The concept of how you can be part of a whole and still an individual is difficult to express because physical reality draws such distinct boundaries in terms of the distinctions between beings. Some people get close when they use the analogy of the Earth being like a single organism. That is something akin to what I am trying to express.

Do not fear for your selfhood. You will never cease to be you, and yet will inexorably become more of the you that now exists as a discrete entity in your own evaluation of your self.

Concerning Leslie's job: she does not like it because she has seen that she is limiting herself. Why, then did she choose it? To show herself that she is limiting herself.

That is a quite fine lesson, then, and she is a quite fine teacher, one who is well versed in the methods of having her student – meaning, her own self – benefit in the best way possible from the "day's lesson."

The reason this issue of limitation is such an important concept right now for her is that she has come to understand herself and her talents better in the past few months. That understanding allows more of the truth to be grasped by her, and the truth concerns her worth to others as well as to herself. In times past, she would have grappled with the issue of her own worth to herself, but now she is moving into a more expansive understanding that is showing her more of her true value to others, particularly to people whose evaluations of themselves are based on lies that have been perpetrated by those around them. I am saying that her current situation is showing her that she is solid in her evaluation of her abilities to add value to others' lives. What better way to make this point than to put oneself into a position where being able to add this value is restricted, as it is with the job in question?

Sometimes the best way to accept a lesson is to put yourself in a place where you do not have the freedom to demonstrate the lesson.

Finally, concerning your development in your mother's womb, your speech difficulties as a child, and your current sleep problems, they are indeed all related. You have correctly seen many of the reasons for why these things have occurred.

One additional thing to consider, though, is the topic of expression. There is no more expressive act than "coming into existence" in the manner that physical birth is a literal expression of that act. There is a connection to expression in the area of speech, obviously. And there is a link to the idea of expression as it relates to sleep because the most unbridled expressions of creativity that occur for physical humans is quite often the dream event.

Now, if you consider the difficulties you have had in these areas, you can see that there is a connection to the concept of "trying to control the freedom of expression" that you have allowed yourself. One of your great lessons in this physical existence is to deal with the issue of allowing yourself the total freedom to which you are entitled. In some past physical lives you were quite wealthy and lacked for nothing. Because, in those existences, you sometimes considered yourself "guilty" for possessing such wealth, you tried to come to grips with that concept in other of your physical lives. One way to assuage guilt is to restrict the acceptance of good things. You have been working to overcome the hesitancy of accepting good things.

You deserve every good thing you get! You deserve them simply because you exist!

Do not worry about a lack of oxygen to the brain. Your sleep cycling difficulties are a way to prompt certain dream experiences. You have to force yourself into this acceptance of expansive dreams because you feel guilty about having the dreams. Don't worry about it! Your decision about how to deal with the physical difficulty is appropriate and will be successful. You will also find that, upon the adjustment of the physical conditions that are connected to the sleep difficulty, you will not have lost the ability to cycle appropriately during sleep in good dream states.

You see, only the true expression of self can lead to perfect fulfillment. Perfect fulfillment of self automatically means perfect fulfillment of others.

Express yourself joyfully. It is okay.

Incidentally, my hearty congratulations on your fine book! Beliefology is a concept whose "time has come, has always been, and will always be." "Spirit", singular, is a better choice – it is closer to the expression in "popular parlance" that will be congruent with the content of your new work.

*Lovingly,
Teach*

❖ ❖ TEACH SESSIONS ❖ ❖

Once or twice a year I write Jeff to ask *Teach* to provide feedback on questions of either a personal nature or a philosophical pondering. It's fascinating to see the difference in the delivery of automatic writing between the hand written dictation of the seventies and what I get now with the advent of modern computer technology. In fact I think on one occasion during a Christmas holiday Jeff/*Teach* responded to my questions via his lap-top computer during an airline flight!

I'm including some of my written correspondence sessions with *Teach* for several reasons. First I want to illustrate how our guides and teachers are there to support us, provide unconditional love and offer guidance, although they do not tell us what to do and they can't do it for us. Another reason is so you can see the common theme that seems to be running through several sessions regarding living naturally, consciously and learning to *allow* things to happen in their own time versus pushing events.

But my most important objective is to share my health challenges and show you how *Teach* assists me in my on-going self discovery process, helping me discover which of my beliefs are creating particular diseases. Remember any illness is merely an outer reflection/manifestaion of an unresolved emotional issue. Humans are energy expressions and whenever we impede the natural flow of energy in motion (*e-*motion) with fear and guilt, we create *dis-*eased bodies, and unhappy *de-*pressed minds. Physical and emotional pain serve as a barameter of your need to transform your thinking and beliefs. Medicine and superficial life changes will only provide temporary relief. Until you resolve the original issue or conflict, you will continue to draw in the same illness or unfavorable events. Observe your pain and it will lead you to your erroneous beliefs. Ignore the pain and what you *resist* will *persist.*

As a teacher I have discovered that it is easier to identify the erroneous and limiting beliefs in others than it is to see them in oneself. Consequently, I'm willing to expose my most personal journeys, hoping that there may be some reader who will read about my discoveries and can discern what is going on in their own *inner* dialogues that may be creating their *outer* life.

Teach 119

Questions: May, 1994

1. After reading Alexander's most recent book *EARTHLY CYCLES* I felt confused about one's individuality and self awareness after the review of the person's "last" life time. Was my perception accurate regarding Alexander's description that once the earth personality dies it processes the life experience and subsequently becomes like a book in the library of life and then the person is more or less absorbed into the entity (oversoul's consciousness)? Is Alexander saying "Don't lose our identity?" This isn't what I feel *Seth* and my teacher *Haré* and the teaching/healing Entities say about reincarnational selves.

One of the many reasons I have an affinity for the *Seth* and *Haré* consciousness illustrations and information is because to me it makes sense that no identity can be lost into some Nirvana or that individuality is a temporary step child of the ego that may be annihilated. Furthermore, I felt that Alexander was essentially stating that the earth personality was more or less under the control of the over soul with minimal purpose and again would be consolidated after it served the entities' purpose. Am I misunderstanding or distorting Alexander message? Please allow me to share my view and please advise me if my concept is off, perhaps my ego is fearful of losing my self-awareness and personal identity individuality.

First of all, it's hard for me to put into words because I agree with *Sethian* philosophy in that all time is simultaneous so therefore Ken is still 5, 15, 30, and on and on, as well as the probability that Ken chose to manifest simultaneous elsewhere. For communication sake, using time, I believe that entities are like corporations, counties, states, or any other organizations consisting of individuals to make up the collective consciousness. Lets say many of these aforementioned organizations are like an entity (oversoul) with a general mission (that is always free to change) with many diverse purposes who hires/recruits (like earth individuals) members who also have their own pursuits and individual missions (that is always free to change). Now it is my belief that death is like a person who has decided that he/she has served their purpose. To use the earlier analogy, they decided to retire from that earth corporation, leaving behind their contributions. But the reincarnated person would continue to be self-aware and have some part of that person's consciousness in order to have an on-going awareness identity that would remember all the other corporations or lifetimes it was living simultaneously. For instance, *Amel* refers to his life in Persia and *Seth* refers to his many different life times so your individual consciousness must continue forever! Aren't time and lifetimes simultaneous?

Isn't death like a vacation or probably it is more appropriate to say like moving from one county to another and never returning to your home land. You leave your family, friends, fellow workers; you can continue to correspond but you are still you except in death it's a transition to a new reality where you no longer require a physical terminal for your Bio-computer. In addition, I felt Alexander's information about Karma was very similar to traditional eastern philosophy and religions. Please comment.

I guess to summarize, I feel that now as well as after our physical death that we are an awarized, conscious, co-creating (with the freedom of choice) individual integral part/member of our overall entity just like Dayton is in Ohio but *not* Ohio; Texas is in the USA but *not* USA, and that if we desired and were knowledgeable and skilled enough, we could branch off and become another separate entity under the ever expanding umbrella of all that is. In other words, we become more and not less!

2. More and more information regarding laser surgery is making the news. Are there laser treatments that could eradicate my bowel problems and obstructive sleep apnea or would it be more beneficial to ascertain the metaphysical cause and to self-care it by resolving the cause? Are there dietary recommendations?

3. My sister is currently in intensive care and not expected to live very much longer even though she was given a death sentence last September and bounced back after spending a week in a coma. Would it be possible for you to assist her and her guides with her transition. Is there any reincarnational insight you can provide that may help me in understanding her life struggles that she brought to herself?

4. Since this session seems to return to reincarnational issues, please, if possible, respond to the following:
    Very few people (especially male), enjoy music from the 30's and 40's and often refer to it as elevator music. I get high (naturally(smile) when I hear tunes such as Moonlight Serenade, Glen Miller, Clair Delune, Debussy, Autumn Leaves, and etc. Is it due to my mother playing music when I was younger, or is there a significant reincarnational life bleeding through from a life time in that era?
    Another possibility is, since I'm an independent thinker/person, could it be I just enjoy the music because I refuse to conform to current fads or be influenced by what each generation dictates should like.

In addition, I always felt I had a counterpart in the Soviet Union struggling with the pursuit of freedom.

5. Can/would you comment on the pro's and con's of self publishing my first book versus submitting it to a publisher like Krammer (*Orin* & *Dabin* Publishers).

TEACH'S ANSWER: May 11, 1994

My Dear Ken,

Concerning your first question, there is always the existence of the individual. It is true that the purposes of the individual's life can mean a moving toward reintegration with the All That Is, and that the individual's growth furthers that process. However, to say that an earthly incarnation is a learning experience with a closing to it is to be inaccurate.

The earthly incarnation is an individuation of the overself, that is true. The purpose for the individuation is for the entire being to learn, grow, create, and fulfill itself. It does this by experiencing in innumerable manners. Corporeal existence is just one of those manners.

What occurs before physical birth is a sort of "conference" between physical-being-to-be and the overself. Certain decisions are made about the best circumstances to learn certain lessons and address certain challenges in the being's overall development. The selection of those circumstances dictates the being-to-be's parents, birth conditions, etc.

It is always the wisdom of self that creates the conditions into which an infant is born.

Once in physical form, the individuated portion of overself that is the physical being beings to learn and grow. If the human incarnation successfully addresses those issues best embodied by the circumstances into which the human was born, then the purpose for that lifetime has been fulfilled.

Now, it may take many lifetimes for one lesson to be completely addressed. This is not necessarily because there has to be a long, drawn-out apprenticeship that must be paid for spiritual awareness. There may simply be many facets to the challenge that require much corporeal time to address.

The reason, of course, that these lessons are addressed in physical reality is because physical reality dictates a time lag between implantation of a belief and the physical creation of reality that manifests as a result of that belief. Without this time lag, there can be confusion about the true source of the spark that defines life; meaning, if instantaneous manifestation occurred in physical reality, there would not be the opportunity for the being to observe the interactions that ripple out from any belief projected outward.

One of the key lessons of physical reality is that no being exists in isolation, and that each being is truly a part of All That Is. Without individuation, which allows a sort of objectivity and "stepping outside of self," that lesson can be lost to camouflage, much as a hidden belief camouflages the real reasons why an individual experiences those conditions that appear in his or her life.

The "book" aspect that Alexander referred to was the Akashic Records aspect of a life lived. There is truly a record of everything that occurs to everybody, and there is no way to prevent that record from being written. It is one result of the impressions left by consciousness of the fabric of space-time-spacelessness-timelessness. Sensitive people who can read the Akashic records can tap into any aspect of any event, past or future, because a record of that event has been left like ripples trailing after a boat moving through the water.

The Akashic record of an individual's life, however, is NOT the individual. It is simply a record. At death the individual re-integrates with the overself, but only after readjustment to non-physical reality. The readjustment period includes the individual remaining as the self-recognized individual until any misperceptions of the afterlife carried over from the physical life drop away (an individual believing himself to be damned to hell for his action in physical life will find himself in an excellent hell immediately after his physical death; after enough reflection on his physical life and lessons learned or missed, he wakes up to the reality of existence and reintegrates with his overself).

The tricky thing to realize, of course, is that all of this happens simultaneously. The individual has not yet been born, and yet has already died.

The universe exists quite nicely in the second of the big bang, and everything that happened in physical reality history already happened in that nanosecond.

True adepts come to understand how to step outside of any physical timeline. That is why they seemingly can manipulate through time. Still, any of their travels are not really through time -- they've simply moved "vertically" instead of "laterally" because they understand the non-linearity of all existence.

To bring this back to the individual's experience, then the individual's life experiences are written in the Akashic Records, not by some scribe, but as a result of the natural process of being that means an individual creates interactions with time/space/other individuals. Those interactions result in "trace patterns within the stuff of reality that forms the psychic library which is the Records." The being that is the individual, however, continues beyond physical death, "eventually" reintegrates with the overself, and another individuation of the overself incorporates via a reincarnational self. The process can continue over thousands of physical lifetimes.

(Please understand, I am using mistranslations of time here. It is unavoidable when describing non-physical occurrences with physical language.)

Eventually, the being learns, grows, creates, and fulfills enough to move beyond further benefit of physical life. That is not to say the being will never be physical again; sometimes, a life is chosen just as a divertissement, for no other reason than that it is fun to experience physicality. The main venue for learning, growing, creating, and fulfilling, however, moves to the non-physical domain, where, for instance, instantaneous manifestation IS the rule. You can see that entirely different lessons would be possible in such environs.

You need never fear the dissolution of self, or anything like a movement into the nothingness of nirvana. That is a distortion. One of the reasons for existence is to celebrate individuality. That individuality takes many forms over many lifetimes. And when all challenges and lessons that physical realities are most appropriate to teach have been addressed, then there is a natural integration of all individuations-that-have-been-and-that-will-be into an expanded overself. That overself then learns its own lessons in its own realities (not that it doesn't learn during the existences of physical individuations, mind you).

It is true that the drive pushing the overself's existence is the drive toward total reintegration with the All That Is. Even this, though, is not a nirvana of nothingness. It is a method for exploring even different ways of being alive.

There can never be an extinguishing of an individual. The oversoul will continue, AND the individual will continue in the expansive simultaneity of time.

Your corporation analogy works in some fashions on some points, but the one thing to remember is that there is never a permanence to death or a physical existence. The true meaning of the simultaneity of time is that there is never a beginning or an end to any stretch of "time". It is simply the physical mechanism of the brain that makes it seem like death occurs because the physical brain is not aware of the many levels of reality. The physical brain also can not grasp the simultaneity of time because it is a corporeal-based mechanism that functions within linear, seemingly cause-and-effect time. From that perspective there are perceived beginnings and ends. A mechanism not based in corporeal reality does not have to deal with that limitation. That is why states of "higher consciousness" breaks down to a certain extent the physical connection to the brain.

Think of the physical brain as a door. A door is a physical thing, yet what is on one side of the door is non-physical. You use a door when you grab hold of the doorknob and pull the door open in order to get a glimpse of the great outdoors (translation: the greater aspects of true reality that exist behind all physical matter).

Now, on the subject of karma, there are many widespread misconceptions. There is no karmic debt that ever need be repaid. Understanding the simultaneous nature of time made this obvious. The concept of repayment is distorted because the concept of guilt is itself a distortion.

If a person acts completely naturally, there is no need for guilt. Only when natural action is quashed is there the development of guilt. Unfortunately, physical reality sometimes requires the suppression of natural action (a three-year-old running gleefully into the street to chase a ball, for instance). This suppression can create guilt (the child feels guilty for disobeying the parent), and then the concept of retribution for the guilty act seems to be a good thing.

The truth is, one incarnation never has to repay another because each incarnation chose and created its own reality as the perfectly natural mean to address the challenges it most needs to experience.

The summary paragraph of your question one is excellent analogy!

The subject of your physical obstructions and the advisability of laser surgery is one deeply rooted in some core beliefs. The first thing of which you must be aware is that both physical conditions to which you allude deal with self-generated obstructions. In other words, your body (translate: you, because your body is the physical manifestation of your beliefs) has itself created impediments to life-giving and life-sustaining functions.

That should be a very clear message to you that there are obstructions of belief to the creation of the life you want.

Look at the physical areas involved for clues about the psychic areas that must be addressed. Your bowel obstruction difficulties are one clear way the body of your *beliefs can send you a message that you possess an impediment to your beliefs of limitation.*

There are responses that should flow through you. The energy of those responses is meant to be freely dissipated. Many times, however, you believe you must be cautious about "giving away" energy. The fact is, the free flow of energy through your life is the only way to have all the energy you'll ever need. You must not worry about hoarding energy or doling it out in precious packets. The energy that creates your life is literally unlimited. Celebrate that fact instead of trying to pinch any energy off as a conservation measure. There are no limitations to the amount of the life force that exists in any being.

The interruption of life-sustaining intake (the air you breathe) also results from a belief of limitation. The limiting belief in this area, however, is a belief in undeservedness. Do some belief work on the issue of deservedness in your life. The truth about what you deserve is that you deserve to have unlimited opportunity and abundance and knowledge and ability to help others. A limiting belief that does not allow that creates conditions under which the body creates impediments to taking in that which is necessary for life.

<u>*Deservedness is key in this area.*</u>

Opting for the surgery may be a good thing IF you also understand that the beliefs still need to be addressed. If they are not changed, your body, of course, will find other ways to draw your attention to these limitations. Given the fact, however, that your body has literally grown certain structures as a result of the limiting beliefs, the time lag between the disappearance of those structures as a result of a change in the core beliefs may be longer than you care to deal with.

It was the appropriate choice that your sister made recently. There was a great lesson learned last fall that happened during the time of her coma on certain levels of her consciousness. The fact that the lesson was successfully completed (and please understand that she and her overself created the lesson as a matter of choice in order to deal with overriding challenges in her development) is the reason she recovered from her "death sentence" at the time.

The awareness that came into her understanding also brought with it, however, an understanding that now that she knew what she did, there were some very exciting and expansive waiting for her in the after-physical-death environment and in other corporeal incantations.

The issues with which she dealt in this lifetime were challenges that she has been dealing with in many physical lifetimes. There was a sort of breakthrough in understanding in this lifetime about the ease of creation, both on a personal and on universal basis. As contradictory as it may appear, she learned that it is easy to exist in a state of natural grace because that state is normal. Suffering is contradictory to that ease, and that is why the coma was a necessary part of the lesson--there was no disease during the coma. Her greater self had the freedom then (without constant physical reminders from the individuation that was dealing most intimately with the challenge at the time) to experience that truth. The only way to get to that truth for her was to break enough of the link to the physical to allow travel to levels where this truth is not subverted by the beliefs that create a limiting corporeal reality.

What she learned during the coma guaranteed that she would soon choose to return to that freedom. It was the appropriate classroom.

There is great joy in her new environs. She is well cared for by herself.

Your music question is very interesting!

First, there is truth in all the possibilities you raise as reasons for your affinity for this kind of music. You did indeed have an incarnation in which you dealt with this music. You were not a composer or performer, however, you were an individual who made his living by selling the music. You sold it because you loved it. You loved yourself because you could see the people who bought it using the music to contribute enjoyment to their lives. You took your own joy in that venture.

You like the music now also because you see yourself as a reactionary in certain ways. This one avenue is very important to send yourself reactionary substantiation because it is so natural for you to enjoy this kind of music, in spite of the fact you are running against the current by having this proclivity.

When a being manifests beliefs, using a natural outlet is always the method of choice. With a natural love of the music, with a "recent" incarnational experience with the music that was empowering, it is no wonder you continue to enjoy these melodies!

Your Soviet counterpart struggles with artistic freedom as well as political freedom. That is another reason for your connection to music of a "reactionary" nature.

(Incidentally, your sensitivity to your Soviet friend is partly due to his culture's much more willing acceptance of the paranormal. With your beliefs about the nature of true reality, it is inevitable that the two of you share information at certain levels much closer to consciousness than the levels on which sharing occurs between two counterparts whose physical manifestations choose to believe there is no such thing as a sixth sense.)

On the subject of publishing your book, the plot of your present now argues for the self-publishing route. Be aware that some of the beliefs that make this your probable course of action are limiting beliefs.

The main limiting belief is that you lack the ability to transmit your message to those who are not predisposed to, or even hostile to, the concept of multidimensionality of self. With that belief, it would be very difficult to pitch your book to the nuts-and-bolts world of bottom-line publishing.

If you change that limiting belief, then not only do you become more effective in landing publishing interest, but you widen the possible audience.

This issue is one of your lessons in this lifetime. It has to do with understanding the commonalty of life. There is, in a very real sense, no such thing as a different human being; every individual human being is a part of the All That Is.

If you look for the similar attributes among those you believe to be different, you will find those same attributes in yourself and all others already believing in multi-dimensional reality.

Now, it could be that self-publishing is one way you come to learn this lesson. It is your choice about which route you choose.

In closing, I applaud your more expansive understanding of self. There is more naturalness to your life now; adjust the beliefs we have discussed, and you will be even closer to the natural state of perfection that is your birthright.

Love,
Teach

The following is a letter in answer to a request about information on several issues.

TEACH'S ANSWER: December 24, 1993

My Dear Ken,

You are moving into a time of change in your life. Much of this change is a result of preparation that you have been making for some time. It is not just you that is making this change--Leslie is changing too. These changes are for the better. They come about because of desires on your part that have been coupled with the understanding of belief adjustments.

First, the recent death of Leslie's father will result in changes for both of you. It already has brought about several changes. Before addressing that issue, however, let me make some comments about why he chose the time and manner of leaving that he chose.

There has always been a belief on his part that it would be wrong for him to linger in death. He was a proud man with a proud concept of life. He felt it was his responsibility to himself and those around him to take care of himself. He was always proud of the ability. For such a person, a life which included long stretches of incapacitation would be anathema. His belief on this issue guaranteed him swift death.

There is nothing wrong in that. Some may think that such a death would rob his loved ones of the change to say good-by. Not so. He made his good-byes on a subconscious basis, in the dream state, and by remaining true to his belief in the rightness of this course of action.

None of you have need of any shock at the situation. On the contrary, you should relax in the knowledge that he was completely content in his choice and timing. Not only was the manner in which he died appropriate for him, but the timing was appropriate also. The time had come when he wished to do some searching in manners not possible in a corporate reality. There are supremely important issues he is dealing with now that involve his continued growth, fulfillment, and creativity. He is, in fact, in the perfect environment to pursue those activities.

He is well. He is happy. He is involved with expanding his understanding of himself. He will take the opportunity to contact the two of you when the time is right. The format of this contact will be in the dream state. Do not be anxious for the contact - it will come at the right time.

The change brought about in your lives as a result of his death occurs in two ways: you are both more intimately connected to life now, and you sense yourselves freed in certain respects to pursue with greater abandon your own interests.

You are intimately connected with life because you sense in a closer-to-conscious way the natural order of things. One of the reasons for your inquiry about your father-in-law's death is that you seek validation for your expanded understanding of the rightness of all existence. Though it is difficult to use words to express the feelings of connectedness with the All That Is, you are starting to sense a more "at ease-ness" with life, with yourself, and with each other. That sensation is one of your greatest *allies* when dealing with this death because there is, in some unspoken manner, an understanding on your parts that there is rightness and an overriding propriety to his death. It is not a resignation, it is an understanding that nature moves with only proper and useful rhythms.

It is the wisdom of the life-force within us that you are allowing yourselves to be more intimately connected to. The reason your father-in-law's death plays a role in that understanding is that you see the rightness of the action from his perspective, and that is an expansive viewpoint.

The freedom I mentioned that is connected with this event is because, finally seeing the propriety of the All That Is as you have forced yourselves to see it as a result of his death, you now see your own actions in a less distorted manner. Seeing your world clearly means you feel more intimately connected to it. That connection gives you the courage to follow your natural course.

What I am saying is that there are many representations you held out for yourselves that were embodied by this parent. With his death, these representations are no longer valid. The biggest of these representations is that you live for yourselves now, that you live for your own expectations, and that you live for your own fulfillments. You would have come to those realizations even without the death, but the realizations would have been delayed.

Now, what I am telling you are things that are going on at levels far below consciousness. It is not a trespass, however, to reveal such things because they would come to you sooner or later, given the paths that you have chosen-- paths where you seek the inner understanding.

This is a good time to begin preparations for your self-employment. One of the reasons has to do with the comments I just made. Another is that you are coming to understand the way to allow your beliefs to work is not to force them to work.

What I mean by that is you have experienced some subtle shifts in your comprehension of how to manipulate your life. Many times before when you attempted belief-change work, you tried to force it to happen. Then you would wait anxiously to try to verify physical results. When the results didn't immediately come, you berated yourself for not "doing it right."

Recently you have come to understand better the naturalness of the process as it is intended to operate. It is truth that many times an individual can not have the reality he desires until he, "stops focusing on it." As contradictory as that sounds, it is common. What is actually happening is that the individual had really learned to stop focusing on the limiting beliefs.

As an example, if someone wishes a great deal of money but finds himself constantly struggling with bills, he will often focus so much on trying to see and experience wealth that what he is really doing is constantly comparing his state with what he wants. That only reinforces the lack.

When the individual instead somehow manages a way to put himself in a situation to at least not be forced to constantly look at his lacks (let us say because he finally lands a job that, while certainly not affording him the ability to buy anything he wants, at least lets him dispense with worry about paying the bills), then he can begin to give himself free rein to let his natural processes bring what he does want to him in a natural fashion. This happens because he is no longer focused on the lacks.

It is not necessary that someone get the job first before the natural way of bringing abundance can be put in place, but in your society with its constant barrage of messages about wealth and lack, it is the very rare individual who can drop the focus on lack without first putting himself in a position that he no longer worrys about a state of lack.

You have maneuvered yourself into just such a position in the past months; you are now, therefore able to more effectively allow the abundance's into your life.

Because this is it, your timeline is a good one. It is also a wise idea to proceed with your book before you make major changes. One of the biggest reasons this is so is because the book will bring some epiphany realizations to you about our own life and about your connection with self and with greater portions of self. Look forward to the epiphany!

Your plan concerning clientele for your services is a good one. You can see the wisdom of appealing to these people when you factor in the understanding about yourself and how you allow a more natural flow to your life to take shape. This more natural flow means you are better able to use those people, places, and events that happen naturally as a part of your world now and as part of the proper way for your life to form itself.

Concerning location, there are some interesting possibilities for you in the Southeast. You will be coming to some understanding about the environments you work best in and your Deservedness to be there. The self-discovery process that I alluded to concerning the production of your book will provide further information about this. For now, where you are is appropriate. More information will come from your own understanding of self when you write your book. Leslie's job search should take her to the education field. There are opportunities for her in education. It is possible that formal education could provide an avenue for her, but because of her belief system, alternative education settings would probably be better. Training programs, education providers who are supplements to formal schooling, education departments within corporations, rehabilitative education, etc. are all sources for her. There is a great wellspring of contribution that resides within her; she simply needs to find that avenue that allows her to function as a teacher in circumstances that fit her own best interests.

Your wife is a marvelous teacher; she will find a way to teach.

Let me close by saying you should congratulate yourself on many understandings about yourself that you have come to recently. You have been living a more natural life, one not so filled with negative focuses. Let it continue.

With Love,
Teach

❖ ❖ ❖ ❖ ❖ ❖ ❖

The following is an excerpt from a Teach session dated November 11, 1994. I'm including this since it pertains to my beliefs and my belief work regarding my health.

TEACH'S ANSWER: November 11, 1994

On another topic, writing is a form of self-discovery. As such it can do nothing but mimic life, because that's what life is. You will find the connections you are noting will continue. It cannot be otherwise.

Acupuncture will be very good for your physical problems. The real issues, of course, are the belief involved.

You have a need to "clear the shit" from your life. You have been holding on to it, and that's not the normal function of a healthy colon.

The shit is a build-up of negative beliefs. You have made progress in the area, for sure, but there is always the impatience that the body had for a return to its natural state.

The reason acupuncture will help is because it will adjust some energy flows. The "damming up: that is symbolic in your disease is also manifesting itself in the flow of energy throughout your body. The acupuncture will address that.

However, the big issue is the belief adjustment. Clear the shit. You have done a certain amount of that, but this is also an area where you have withheld judgments about yourself. As a consequence, you have harbored certain feelings that should be allowed to flow freely.

    Look for those feelings. One of them is the feeling of independence. You have told yourself there are some negative consequences to independence, and you have stopped up your natural inclination toward independence as a result.

    As you can see, the issue of independence will be a prominent one as you move into your new situation. For that reason also, you should address your beliefs about independence.

    As do most people in your society, there is a conscious desire for independence. Also, as with most people, there is a certain fear of it. There is some of that fear in your beliefs. Examine the issue of relationships as they pertain to independence. You will find some hidden beliefs that act to quash the successful reach to independence.

    These beliefs are also quashing the normal function of your ability to have life flow freely through you.

    As always, I am confident of your growth and the continued ability you possess to better your circumstances.

    Lovingly,
    Teach

142 INTERNAL LIFE

As you read this next letter, you will notice several references to *Framework 2*. Framework 2 is a term *Seth* uses to describe the inner dimensions of physical realities or what I refer to as the cosmic internal casting studio in another chapter. *Seth* states that Framework 2 is the origin for the energy and power in our day-to-day world that he calls *Framework 1*. According to *Seth*, all details for our life are arranged in Framework 2, including the so called coincidences. Furthermore, *Seth* says that Framework 2 is responsible for the inner maintenance and mechanisms for body functions such as respiratory, elimination and heart/circulatory systems.

TEACH'S ANSWER: May 28, 1995

My Dear Ken,

First, you know your contact with Haré is dependable and brings you excellent information. The information provided certainly falls into that category. There is one thing of which you should be aware, however. Your personal contact is always the source that will provide the most helpful and the most useful information.

Congratulations on having the kind of contact that can bring you such excellent information.

It is true that alien intelligence's are fact, not fiction. They do not exist in physical reality in the same manner humans do, however. The references to Alexander's' statements are true: often a UFO sighting is brief bleed through from another reality. That is why the motions made by the supposed UFO do not seem to follow the laws of physics as they exist in your reality. The UFO, being a bleed through from another reality, acts in concert with the laws of motion in its own reality. That reality may contain different "laws of physics" than your own.

Many people place constraints on knowledge. They operate out of a mindset that says two opposing things cannot both be true. What is often happening in such an instance is that there are not two different things occurring; there are two manifestations of the same thing occurring.

It is like someone looking at an apple and saying, "I see the top, so I cannot see the bottom at the same time." The whole apple can be viewed if the individual steps back and refocuses.

That is what happens sometimes when one statement is heard and then another, equally true statement is heard which seems to contradict the first. The old story of the blind man describing the elephant works beautifully as a teaching device. One person, seeing the top of the apple, would describe it quite differently from someone seeing only the bottom of the apple.

Alexander's comments can be an apple stem; another's comment can be an apple core, or the apple skin, or the meat of the apple. They are all accurate descriptions of the apple.

Now, some UF-Ologists would say non-physical bleed through is the only way contact occurs from extraterrestrials. Others would say alien abductions are the form of contact. There are many different forms that can occur, and every form would seem to have its proponent.

When humanity accepts the broader view - the much broader viewpoint - humans will see that aliens represent only a different part of the whole of consciousness. Now, the current thinking happens to be based from a human-centric viewpoint. That is the reason "alien" is the description used.

When the truth becomes known - that human and "alien" are just different parts of the same big whole of consciousness and sentience - then the recognition of contact will become commonplace.

It is easy to see, however, that such a mass psyche mindset is nowhere close to existing now. That becomes very clear when one looks at the difficulties caused by humans who carry beliefs that other humans are "less then human." Witness the massacre of thousands of one tribe simply because they weren't of the same tribe as those doing the slaughtering.

It is any wonder there is not an acceptance of aliens? Something as minor as the color of one human's skin is enough to cause some humans to hate others. What would those people do if they suddenly found themselves in a society with intelligent, conscious beings who were much different then merely a human with a different skin color?

It would not be pretty.

The truth, then, is that until humanity can accept itself as only one part of consciousness and sentience, and understand that its one part is interdependent on the whole, humans will never accept the existence of alien beings.

Some humans are not threatened by this mindset. Most humans cannot handle it.

Have other races included what would be termed by a human observer as a reptilian being? Absolutely. Humans judge others by the only standards they know how to use: humans' standards (and many humans fall woefully short on those standards!).

So, your information is accurate. How different people will judge it can cause wide variations in the supposed "accuracy" of the material, however.

Leslie's mother is indeed making certain decisions. For one with her belief system, it is a very difficult thing to be without her husband. there is a great dependence on the necessity of the "rightness" of things for her. Her sense of order comes when things are "right." Being without her husband is not "right"

Given the conditions of her early years and the interaction with her caregivers' (translation: belief-installers), there is a necessity to be with her husband. It is the proper thing for one with such a belief system.

This kind of belief system functions quite appropriately when the husband is around. When he is gone there are some difficulties. One of the greatest of those difficulties is the identification of the rightness of self.

Leslie's mother does not currently believe she is "right" to exist without her husband. Certainly she is not so far on that continuum as, say, an Indian wife who believes she should die when her husband dies, but she does equate her identity with being a wife to her late husband. Having her husband taken from her has caused a very severe jolt to her belief system.

She is currently "in a fog." This is a very common phenomenon when an emotionally impactful event occurs that causes a re-evaluation of beliefs. I have often used the example of someone who identifies strongly with his job suddenly being fired after 20 years of loyal services to the company. That person walks around "in a fog" for a period of time. The assumptions upon which life had been built have been rudely taken away, and until a new set of beliefs is instilled, or a different way to function with the same set of beliefs is found, the individual will be disoriented.

In many instance's disorientation can lead to depression. There is a sense of hopelessness when formerly rock solid assumptions are shown to be inaccurate.

Leslie's mother can make a choice. She can decide to keep her old belief system, not find a way to be a wife to her husband, and die because there is no reason to live. She may, however, find a way to keep the belief system and find another husband (if that is acceptable to that belief system). Her most empowering choice, of course, would be to alter her belief system so that her value to herself is the item that is emphasized.

Given the current plot of the present (the same total of her beliefs), she is predisposed to being blind to ways out of her predicament. This is a challenge she will have to face.

You and Leslie have been supportive and have done all the "right" things. The choice is hers.

Your mother is also making a decision. Her decision about how to cope with her infirmity is very difficult. On the one hand she would like to believe there are ways to live a fulfilling, useful life into very old age, but the information and the prognoses from the medical community lead her to believe that is not possible.

Your mother's situation is a perfect example of someone being hypnotized. She is hypnotized by the beliefs she has chosen to accept. Your medical community has been very successful in spreading its belief system, and most people in your society take medical decrees as gospel. She is such a person.

People who do this find themselves in a quandary when the proclamations from the medical community are discouraging. One reason such proclamations are accepted so uncritically is the belief that inner knowledge is not available. Your mother believes this.

The Native Americans believed in the acceptability of inner knowledge. Their cures would be laughed at by many of your medical practitioners. A large portion of those who don't laugh contain their mirth because they believe there must be something in the herbs and natural remedies the Native Americans used that can be likened to wonder drugs.

There are very few people in the medical community who believe the Native Americans were successful because they ministered to the beliefs held by the body, as opposed to simply ministering to the body by doing things to it or giving it "natural drugs."

In such a belief system as that maintained by the Native Americans, the acceptability of inner knowledge is a common occurrence. For your mother, this acceptance is not allowed because she believes she does not have the training and intelligence and wisdom that doctors have, *therefore, she should not have the temerity to suggest she knows better than they.*

This is in line with her beliefs. She has always been one to trust outside authority more than that supplied by her own inner self. This trait is now causing great problems because it puts her at the mercy of the medical establishment.

In most cases, arthritis is a statement made by the body that there is a longing for movement. This movement is not necessarily physical, but the body must speak with the only language available to it. In your mother's case the movement that is needed is movement of spirit.

She longs for a situation in which her spirit can soar. She has seen opportunities for that become less and less. One of the reasons is her evaluation of technology as something that necessarily prevents the expansion of spirit. Another reason is her belief that a certain age brings with it diminished opportunities for soaring.

Her arthritis would improve if she allowed a great work of art, for instance, to move her. Notice the emphasis on the word move - it is not just a play on words. She would feel much better if she were moved emotionally in joyous ways.

She should be active with her spirit; it must be unfettered. She is lassoing it with her arthritis (and vice versa).

She can improve by choosing to do these things. You can assist by allowing her that freedom.

You have the right idea when you think in terms of "allowing" yourself more freedom regarding your timeline for making the transition to a different vocation. It is no coincidence you choose to think in those terms. Such language reflects the change in thinking that goes along with the concept of giving yourself freedom.

One of your greatest challenges has been in accepting the natural flow that is possible when you accept the rightness of self. You are the kind of person who likes to tinker with things, trying to make things "just so," attempting to "cover all the bases." This is a good thing in many ways. In some ways, however, it crimps your ability to allow natural perfection.

Framework 2 is totally benevolent, so any creations coming from it are always going to be beneficial. There is no need for fine-tuning because perfection exists as it is created in Framework 2 and then makes its way into reality. This is the way an animal, for instance, can function with such beauty and yet depend only on instinct to function at all. Animals do not have the conscious mechanism to allow goal choices on a grand scale, but they succeed wonderfully by trusting only the wisdom of Framework 2.

Humans, on the other hand, can do the same thing, but rarely do. They prefer, in many instances, to force the consciousness to do that which it was never intended to accomplish: to figure out how to attain the goal at every step in the process.

If you consider what is necessary to accomplish anything, there are innumerable steps. Most people aren't aware of all the steps because most of the beginning steps are invisible to them. the beginning step of writing a novel, for instance, might be, "to see the blank piece of paper with one's eyesight." That is truly one of the steps, but most writers never even consider it. They don't consider it *because it is a "given", something they spend no thought on because it is taken for granted.*

Every step can be accomplished in the same manner. It takes the "faith to move mountains" to function in that manner, however.

Now, certainly the consciousness is meant to provide answers to steps in the process. Your scientists put men on the moon by using their consciousness to figure solutions to challenges. Before there was any hope whatsoever of getting to the moon, however, there was an assumption it was achievable. That assumption put into motion certain perfection of the human spirit that allowed the project to overcome massive technological challenges. Those challenges were met because, at some level, there was an assumption that the answer would come.

That is the way it should be in any goal-seeking enterprise. The difficulties arise when there is no assumption the goal is achievable, yet there is still the belief that the consciousness is the means for finding answers.

You do that sometimes.

Here is what happens: you depend too much on your conscious evaluations as the only trustworthy routes to solutions. Now, this may sound strange for someone who deals with non-physical entities in his work, but is true nonetheless. You are a translator, and many times you try to translate inner knowing into a three-dimensional, grounded-in-physical-reality interpretation. That is why you focus so much on timelines and on target dates. You are a kind of project manager for the flow of your life.

This is not altogether bad. It serves you well in certain instances. You have come more and more to understand that it has its limitation, though. That is why you've used the terminology "allowed" in describing how you will accomplish your vocational transition.

Understanding this about yourself means you will recognize the progress you have made in this area. For that reason, it can be only a positive step that you have become less stringent with your timeline. Congratulations!

You are also wise in selecting someone with a very different viewpoint to edit your work. It will be very enlightening to hear comments from such a viewpoint.

There is something more important about the choice, however. You need to depend on the expertise of diverse kinds of people to help you succeed with this venture. It is important as a means of offering you some stability for this reason: your past successes have been built in ventures in which you worked with people, both as your "means of delivery" and as your "product".

In other words, you have a track record of success in a business built on the interaction of people with people. Many of those people held widely divergent views from your own, some so widely divergent that a good portion of humanity would judge them to be deficient in many of the basic human capacities.

The point is, you worked successfully with different kinds of people from yourself. You succeeded where others would not have been able to in that venture because you saw those different kinds of people as a resource. If you go into a business that does not involve a rainbow of personalities, you will feel like a fish out of water. For that reason, selecting someone with a much different background and belief system to be such an integral part in the creation of your books is a positive.

Trust your abilities to create from vastly differing mixes of people, opportunities, and raw materials. You are someone who chokes on homogeneity. So long as you don't try to nit-pick the process consciously, you will be successful.

Communication consciously with your father is something not in accordance with your belief system at this time. This is a perfect example of a conscious dependent on process when natural dependence is what is necessary. If you desire this as a goal, then stop your conscious concern for it. Communication on your end is already possible. The phone, in other words, has been installed in your house. You have demonstrated your ability to communicate with non-physical sources of information, as your excellent communication with your greater portions of self has demonstrated. Therefore, there is nothing else to be done on your part. The ball is in his court, but your concern that you want to tell him certain things (resulting from understandings of yourself that did not exist when he was alive) makes the communication desirable on your part. When you accept that such communication will happen when and if he wants it, you will be much closer to making the connection.

Incidentally, it is something that is possible. Content yourself that you have done everything necessary to "allow" it to happen (and see the smile on my face as I use the word around which much of the information you have chosen to teach yourself with these questions is predicated).

Your sister is adapting to her surroundings. She, too, will communicate in the same manner - when there is volition on her part.

You are a good friend, and I am honored to communicate with you. I am honored that one such as you chooses to solicit my opinions. Your own greater self is the wise one in this communication triangle. Listen to that source - you will find enormous wisdom there.

With Love,
Teach

TEACH'S ANSWER: December 29, 1995

My Dear Ken,

There is one very important thing of which to be aware concerning the timeline of your books: there are some things you will learn during the books' production that will be very valuable for inclusion. This means, of course, that some adjustments will need to be made as you come to certain discoveries in you own inner life that merit inclusion in the books.

The lesson from understanding this is that you should be alert for the learning experiences of your life that will occur in the next few weeks. Some of them are highly appropriate for Beliefology. Do not, therefore, pressure yourself with an absolute deadline that exists at the expense of the inclusion of some material that will be very helpful to many people if it is included in the book.

In particular, you're thinking in the lessons you are teaching yourself as you go through a job change and the creation of the book itself are excellent sources of material and inspiration for topics to be discussed in the book. You can see, obviously, how such topics are intimately tied to the subject of beliefs and how individuals use them.

A natural timeline, then - one that unfolds in a manner that allows for sufficient input from your discoveries about yourself - is the best one. Do not fear that such an approach will overly delay finishing the book or jeopardizing any dated commitments for the book's production or distribution. I merely make the point in order to alert you to some opportunities to increase the book's usefulness to its readers as a result of your own lessons learned during the next weeks and months.

Your understandings about yourself concerning money, bank loans, house purchases, etc., are very astute. There is the need for you to feel secure in the belief-change involving money. In your past, you have had struggles to create the proper belief concerning money, and you now are in a much better place with respect to having the appropriate beliefs. You sense, however, a need for a kind of "setting in" with a belief. That is your inner knowledge giving you a clue that the "acclimation" period is still underway.

When beliefs are changed, there is generally a "lag period", that is, a corporeal time span between the belief change and changed physical circumstances that reflect the change in beliefs. This time lag is simply a result of the way the inner world is transformed to the outer, physical world as a result of beliefs being powered into three-dimensional reality, In other words, the time lag is a natural, correct, wonderful, inevitable process.

The inner self, knowing such a time lag must occur and understanding that one of the purposes for the lag is to allow assimilation of the new beliefs on the part of the individual doing the belief change, depends upon the time being there and uses it for many important purposes. There are usually very specific reasons an individual's inner self circumvents this process in those rare situations. Beliefs and physical reality change. Those specific circumstances do not exist for you (as is the case in almost all circumstances). Therefore, you need the "acclimation" time. That is what you have sensed. This means that your purchase of a new home, if that is the course you choose, should be done within circumstances that are most comfortable for you with your feelings concerning your new beliefs. If you are comfortable with saying to yourself, "I know my beliefs have changed and I am now most comfortable just adjusting to those beliefs before testing them," then you should arrange house purchasing based on your comfortable knowledge that such a thing is easiest given a financial background showing current employment other than self-employment.

On the other hand, you can find a suitable house for rent.

And the Southeast is certainly still a delightful area of the country for you. There are certain conditions, climate-wise, that make this case. North Carolina is one area that would be suitable, but there are others.

Of course, the things you move with you are more important that the place to which you move. If you bring appropriate beliefs, you will find a suitable place and home, and you will serve yourself and others very successfully.

You had a brush with a type of "other self" when you met Kim. You are not counterparts, but you share many experiences and several lifetimes. You recognized an "old friend" that popped into this physical lifetime, and you knew much about your old friend.

That is why you had such dependable insight into her situation.

Some of the lifetimes you shared were lives in which both of you were black. One of them was during the eighteenth century as slaves in America. The issues dealt with then concerned the ability to triumph over depression (slavery would certainly be a setting guaranteed to engender a certain amount of depression). You and your friend fought that battle in that life, and Kim's reappearance reminded you, on an unconscious level, of that struggle.

You were more successful in addressing that belief than Richard (then Kim's name) was. The reappearance of Kim/Richard into your current reality is meant to give you some reassurance about the rightness of your new beliefs about your power to create, because you can see the physical reality results of Kim's experience which do not include (to the same extent) those beliefs.

You should thank your old friend - she/he has reappeared to say, "Congratulations. I celebrate your success and take heart from it to continue my own journey." Both of you are helping each other.

Leslie's belief, of course, factored into the upcoming employment termination of her job. There is not a need, however, to agonize over what the beliefs are that brought about the situation. The fact is, the situation is a proper thing given her current beliefs. There is a desire for growth that is a reflection of expanding beliefs. The situation will allow from some of that growth.

There is no way for me to overemphasize the following point: this is a positive development. There are very, very deep and expansive riches of self-determination that Leslie possesses. Her role in the current circumstances is an opportunity to be more connected to that resource.

Leslie's path right now is fairly straightforward. The beliefs that have created the situation also guarantee re-employment. All that is necessary in this situation is for Leslie to carry that conscious understanding with her as she begins the search for other employment. She will be surprised (though not really shocked when she evaluates for strengths and her abilities) at the ease with which another job appears. The bonus is that she will find ways to enrich herself in the new job that did not exist in her current employment.

This is a natural evolution. Both of you should enjoy the growth.

You are absolutely right on your assessment about your health issues. What you are doing now is living in your physical reality some of the things that you have not allowed yourself to live in your internal reality - the ability to let life flow through you without the need to hoard things as a cache against lack. In many ways your internal problems were a reflection of that belief.

When you created physical difficulties, they were, in most instances, related to the idea that you had to conserve, to be miserly with, to hold on to with all diligence, things in your life because you were not capable of generating those things in a natural, self-deserved way. You comment about your trust-love-belief in yourself is a very big change from the old belief. The physical reality of your body's condition will change so that your earlier problems no longer exist when your body (acting as a result of the directions given by beliefs) is convinced of your trust in it and in your ability to have what you deserve. When your body understands that you really believe that, it will no longer feel that need to try to conserve air/fluids/solids by holding on for fear that you will not get enough as a natural course.

Trust your ability to have all that you need. Also understand that you're having all that you need is a natural *process for helping and serving others in the way that is your natural rightness.*

Teach

As in the previous letters of 5/11/94 and 12/29/95, in this next letter *Teach* talks about how my physical body reflects the inner state of my psychic self-image. *Seth* has stated that the ego is a natural part of the physically actualized self. The purpose of the ego is to assist the self to navigate in physical reality. However, difficulties set in when the ego becomes rigid or fearful and attempts to block out other parts of the whole inner self and consequently impedes or blocks vital energy, information, solutions and wisdom from the source or inner self. *Teach* has helped me identify my limiting beliefs about scarcity and deservability in relation to my health and flow of energy. Remember, beliefs are emotionally charged thoughts that have electrical energy and are automatically translated into physical matter by certain parts of the subconscious. These beliefs, accepted by my ego, have disrupted my natural, automatic flow of energy to my body.

As you read the following *Teach* letter, please think of your own beliefs in reference to your life challenges, especially in relation to how people often move beliefs around. I still find it fascinating that as I was making significant progress in the financial arenas of my life, I was simultaneously sabotaging health areas because of similar beliefs, like scarcity and deservability, that previously blocked the flow of financial abundance. It is important to accept ownership and responsibility for creating the unfavorable events and conditions in your life. Unfortunately, many times we refuse to accept our role in attracting certain things and blame other outside influences or even simply ignore the circumstances hoping they will remedy themselves. It is equally important not to mistake responsibility with guilt and blame, thus making situations worse or drawing in other detrimental situations. During the process of transforming your limiting beliefs, remember it is important to *live* and *accept* yourself unconditionally. Allow your emotions to flow and trust that your inner subconscious self will deliver only the best.

TEACH'S ANSWERS: December 26, 1996

My Dear Ken,

There is something very important in your own evaluation of your circumstances - you are seeing the impact of beliefs before they are manifested physically. For instance, you are aware of an individual's belief in scarcity and you see how that belief will be made physical. Another example: you see how your own belief in the rightness of natural living is the feeling about your life that brings you the physical circumstances you desire.

In both these examples you are glimpsing the future. What makes the process dependable is the simultaneity of time. Seeing accurately the various probable futures that stretch out before you, however, is something that is dependent on an acceptance that such seeing is natural and is proper. When one lives naturally, following impulses from Framework 2, there is what many have termed the "expansive now" that is the state of normalcy. The expansive now allows vision of both past and future as well as present.

Sensing the expansive now requires a so-called altered state of consciousness, according to your scientists. The key is, however, that such a state is not altered - it is a natural state into which humans can place themselves at will. Native American shamans, for instance, can do this and expect to do it as part of their commune with the All That Is.

The point is that being in the state in which you glimpse and experience the expansive now is not any alteration if you truly live naturally. It is only the programming that humans have accepted that prevents them from experiencing the expansive now on a regular basis. The ability is latent; it is literally programmed into your genes and into the coding for chemical reactions that must take place in the brain in order to experience the state.

Now, you are beginning to taste the expansive now from time to time. When you do, and when you do not carry limiting beliefs into the experience, you get sensations about probable realities that are occurring in the "future" part of the expansive now. You are beginning to trust those sensations, primarily because you have begun to accept perfection.

Please spend some time playing with the idea of perfection. The truth is, every circumstance and/or experience you encounter is absolutely perfect for your growth and development based on the beliefs you possess at that time!

This means that what has occurred in your past - the past that you now consciously recall - everything in that past - was perfect. All events were perfectly constructed and experienced as the very best things that could have happened to you in order for you to learn, grow, create, and fulfill yourself.

When someone understands the natural perfection of what has been, and will be, experienced, that person can begin to use experience of the expansive now to accelerate the circumstances that continue to provide perfection.

You have, in times past, looked at your corporeal past and bemoaned certain events. You have wondered how it can be possible that experiencing the pain you experienced was perfect. Your experience when you have such considerations is the same as the way most people evaluate their lives - they do not see "the big picture". The "big picture" is another term for the expansive now.

More recently, however, you have been more philosophical about your corporeal experiences. You have allowed yourself greater freedom to examine the events of your life from the perspective of gauging how those events have woven together to create the current you, which is an absolutely perfect representation of your beliefs. The process is vitally important for understanding the effect of beliefs in physical creation, and you are beginning to understand that at the interior body level as well as at the conscious level.

The reason I speak about your tastes of the expansive now is because it is important for you to understand the beautiful naturalness and ease with which you can be the architect of your own life. When you experience the expansive now, you see the events and objects that do not add to your fulfillment, in spite of what your prior beliefs told you! For many people, such recognition is cathartic. Yours has been a more subtle infusion of the understanding due to your conscious predisposition to the truth about the nature of reality.

Nonetheless, you have tasted the expansive now and have started to trust it as the truth.

Now, the intuitions you have about your business partners are beginning to be recognized as a result of living in the expansive now. The intuitions have always been there, of course, but they have been misinterpreted in the past on occasion. Such misinterpretation is impossible in the expansive now because the entire picture of your life is on the canvas, including your intuitions and beliefs. Seeing those together is always instructive because you see the connection between them as a result. The connection is that good intuitions follow good beliefs and inaccurate interpretation of intuitions follow limiting beliefs.

Notice that I said inaccurate interpretations of intuitions. I phrased it that way because the inherent rightness of every living thing, including human beings, guarantees that natural intuitions which, if followed, always lead to the proper growth, will always be present as a baseline of experience. Those intuitions and impulses are the vehicles for the emergency into physical reality that drive into your corporeal existence from their source in Framework 2.

Your intuitions and impulses are always good - that's the underlying rightness of existence asserting itself. Those intuitions and impulses, however, are quickly squashed in most young children's experiences because they are "instructed" by adults in belief-limiting fashions.

When you deal in the expansive now, however, you can only observe true intuitions and impulses, meaning those intuitions and impulses that are naturally a part of the way your consciousness and physical body move into corporeal reality. That process, when allowed its total freedom, results in natural perfection.

    Thus far, your experience of the expansive now has been mostly a non-consciously generated event. Your intuitions, you see, have been allowed enough free rein to bring glimpses of the expansive now to you of their own accord. In time you will be able to consciously initiate experience in the expansive now. Do not try to rush it - it will come. As you inevitably move toward that time, savor the experience whenever it comes as a result of finally having an unimpeded route unfold within your consciousness.

    So, this long introduction has been to explain why I make the following statement: you are accurate in your observations and resulting feelings about your business circumstances and your business partners. Yes, there are belief limitations concerning scarcity on Tom's part that will hamper the full flowering of the business. Yes, there are beliefs possessed by Jim that drive actions on his part demanding retribution toward him (that retribution coming in the form of self-inflicted punishment, though physical circumstances, when examined from a purely corporeal and rational perspective, would lead most people to say certain actions on his part brought about the circumstances he suffers). Jim's actions to attract retribution are his perfection right now because he is teaching himself lessons about the main reason he chose this particular corporeal reality, and part of his retribution toward self quite naturally takes the form of physical expression in his body.

The body is the physical manifestation of belief; it can be no other way.

Your education venture fits your beliefs about helping others, therefore it is a positive, affirming thing for you. There is much good you will do in that venture.

As you begin, let all the opportunities for the success of the venture come into your life. Because the venture is a naturally aligning physical circumstance in your corporeal reality, the events that will bring it into full flowering are already occurring in the expansive now. All that you must do to bring those events from the expansive now into your corporeal reality is to allow them to happen. That means trusting implicitly that they are your perfection.

You have no need to prescribe specific to yourself - doing so only derails the process.

I mention this because there are other sources of funds for you to launch your venture than the one source in front of you. The quick, easy, natural, and joyous way to experience the receipt of those funds is to dismiss thoughts and worries about them happening in your life. The belief in your own individual truth and perfection will attract them to you quickly.

Your phrase, "until my other seeds are ready to harvest," is delightful. It speaks of an inevitability about the circumstance.

That is truth.

Do I have a belief in lack of input to my physical body? Ask yourself that question. It will lead you to discoveries about lessons you are teaching yourself through the mechanism of your physical body.

You have dealt successfully in many areas of your life with the issue of abundance. One of the areas in which the belief still takes hold is in the function and condition of your body. Though you are not aware of it, you are presenting lacks to your body that are resulting in lingering health issues.

The lack is not in the amount of what you eat. The lack is produced by how you eat and what you eat. Your body is sending messages that it needs certain things it is not getting. Unconsciously, you have been creating the lack in order to teach yourself lessons about the consequences of unnatural lack.

That is precisely what is happening now. The body's requirements are natural. When you do not provide those requirements, an unnatural dynamic is initiated. Without the naturalness of the incoming required nutrients, the body attempts to right itself by making adjustments in an effort to exist without the nutrients.

The main point here is not so much trying to figure out which nutrients are lacking in your body as to realize that you can be just as successful dealing with the limiting beliefs of scarcity as it manifests in your body as you have been when the manifestation has presented itself in other areas of your life.

Working on beliefs is an ongoing process. It is possible to completely eliminate limiting beliefs, and that is always the best thing. In the process of doing so, many people often "move beliefs around" as they manipulate them in their procedure for getting rid of them entirely. That is what you have done with your belief about scarcity. The belief still hangs on, though you should relax and feel good about the fact that your past work on the matter and the summation of your other beliefs means that you will soon completely eliminate the limiting beliefs.

Thank yourself for having had it, though, because you learned much as a result of dealing with it.

Accept the fact that learning the truth about yourself is going to mean eradication of undesired physical ailments. That process is in place, is ongoing, and will result in physical health as you desire it. You have laid the foundation for the natural unfolding of the event.

In the meantime, sending your body a message that there is wonderful abundance available to it will be helpful. Again, such abundance is decidedly not in terms of the amount of food. It is manifested by providing your body with supplemental nutrition because you are not currently providing the needed nutrition of your diet.

Leslie's job search has been dependent, at her choice and initiation, on things which do not have to figure into the process. By that I mean the beliefs of others that she has allowed into her reality of the search. One of those people is you.

I am not saying you are limiting her or delaying her success. I am saying she will be successful when she stops including the needs and desires of others into her motivation for securing a job. The job she will get is hers now in the expansive now. It is perfection for her. Because it is that, there is no reason to consider anyone else's beliefs about what she should do or be but her own. Doing so will bring her the greatest fulfillment.

This means Leslie's search will bring her perfection as soon as she dispenses with any thoughts about a job needing to be anything other than what will bring her total happiness.

All other considerations about where to look for a job, what kind of job it should be, what the salary of the job must be, etc., only prevent natural perfection from occurring.

In closing, congratulate yourself at the end of this year for all the strides you have made in living the natural life. You are not consciously aware of all of them simply because you have not looked for them. Look for them! You will find such evidence in many areas of life, and you should give yourself that gift because it will accelerate your total acceptance of the rightness of your physical existence, in all of its various modes of expression.

Lovingly,
Teach

Chapter 11
Internal life

In order to attempt to comprehend the importance, as well as the magnitude, of internal life, we must consider the source, creator and sustainer of not only our universe, but all universes — physical and non-physical. This macrocosm some refer to as *God* and others refer to as *ALL THAT IS*, actualizes, nourishes and germinates itself in all of it's microcosmic creations. Each person, tree, plant and animal is couched within *ALL THAT IS* (*God*), which is likened to an enormous, limitless, cosmic nesting doll. If humankind could only understand this incomprehensible vastness, the immensity of this permanent and eternal love energy transformation with all of it's limitless possibilities, maybe then we would not limit ourselves. For we are not separate, but a living thought-formation, an integral part of this larger and greater gestalt. We are a part of this permanent and eternal, yet simultaneously ever-expanding, ever-changing, ever-growing, pure unconditional love energy essence. *God* cannot be extracted from any atom or creature, and each individual has its own independent identity that can be transformed but never extinguished.

God spawns entities — of which we are a part — similar to the way parents birth children. The parents provide the DNA and the genetics as well as the subsequent love, compassion and nurturing. Like *God*, the parents can guide, direct and love their offspring, but cannot interfere or invade the free will or integrity of each individual consciousness. In other words, each atom, creature and human has total autonomy with it's own uniqueness and identity complete with a conscious desire to know and fulfill itself. As much as parents can want their child to be healthy, happy and responsible, it is totally up to their offspring to eventually find their own purpose. Because of the protective consciousness of *ALL THAT IS*, not even parents can interfere with the growth or free will of their loved ones. Therefore, the purpose of this infinite, inexhaustible, all powerful loving *God* and all of it's simultaneous creations — including humans — is to express itself in limitless creativity, create, enjoy and experience all of its creations.

These entities that are extensions of *ALL THAT IS* (*God*) are psychic energy essences with full conscious gestalt personalities. Then, like a cosmic amoebae, the entities expand and new independent personalities develop. Consequently, these interdependent individuals have autonomy and will create mental and psychic dreams whose ideas will electromagnetically take physical forms. If the new original personalities happen to be human, their mental, emotional and psychological ideas and images will be projected into physical or mental environments. Therefore, all dreams take on their own lives and will take root in some reality — physical or non-physical. Einstein even proclaimed that energy could be transformed but not destroyed.

Internal Life 171

Taking into consideration entity structures, you are only one representative of what my spirit teachers refer to as your *over-soul, whole self,* or *entity*. Everything that exists, physical and non-physical, consists of consciousness that cannot be eradicated, only transformed. Although consciousness always creates form — your overall entity — it is more than consciousness. In seminars, I use the analogy of our entity being like an international organization whose membership includes people of many races and religions. Collectively, this conglomerate has it's overall mission, purpose and creative pursuits, while each individual personality has it's own unique desires, purposes, imagination and development.

So this entity, or you may say *over-soul* if you choose, contains within it all of it's reincarnated selves that had their lifetimes in physical existences, as well as other personalities that were never physical. I often use the example that our soul is like a conscious, living, divine computer and our earthly psyche/personality is just one software program among thousands of other programs. Unlike computers, souls have free-will personalities. They have feelings and are much more aware, cognitive and reflective. Although everything has consciousness — atoms and molecules are simple forms of consciousness — and everything is composed of awarized energy, souls are a much more complex and less limited psychic gestalt.

Historically, scientists have studied nature and humans by examining their exterior. Future practitioners will realize the only way to discover the *BIG PICTURE* is to observe everything from it's entirety. The source and cause of all outside physical manifestations, as well as psychic phenomenon, rises up from internal life. All life — plant, human and animal — is an emotional manifestation of awarized energy that transforms to an outer representation emerging from inner psyche imaginations. Future scientists will not only be examining the inner spirit of nature and it's creatorhood, but more importantly, will be feeling nature's heart. Although on different levels, plants, animals, rocks and dirt have consciousness too, and their desiring spirit dreams them into physical existence from the same internal source from which we come. Consequently, humankind not only creates its own drama, but also is emotionally connected with every particle of nature.

So each entity is a simultaneous by-product of *ALL THAT IS (God)* whose purpose is to express itself creatively by creating and exploring as many realities as it chooses. Say your entity wanted to experience life on the earth plane during the twentieth century. In order to explore the adventure of humankind as both male and female, as well as a variety of races and nationalities, your *over-soul* selects the following: one reincarnated self carefully chooses a family in America in 1998 and decides to be a black male; another identity with this entity's family of consciousness chooses to be Caucasian and agrees to be born female to a single woman in a Scandinavian country in 1953; yet another multi-dimensional self within this collective entity's consciousness is attracted to a poverty-stricken part of Africa where he becomes a starving child; and another emissary selects an extremely opulent existence as a white female in a wealthy French family. Each earthly counterpart has it's own identity, purpose and personal desires and characteristics, but nevertheless, is a part of the same *over-soul.* This same entity simultaneously has reincarnated lifetimes not only in earth existences, but also on other planets and existences in completely different dimensions. Therefore, each life or human expression is fulfilled while it contributes to the overall growth, fulfillment and enjoyment of the entity at-large.

Internal Life

There is absolutely *NO* limit to the expansion, growth or creations of this entity. Just as the entity at-large has unlimited freedom, each lifetime expression is also free to choose as much as it believes in with intrinsic autonomy. Historically, most people who believe in reincarnation believe that each lifetime happens in consecutive order, one after the other. I subscribe to the belief in simultaneous time — that time, space and distance are a factor on the physical plane but that *real* reality is outside of time and space. Thus, in actuality, while all of your lifetimes are happening at once, on earth we can only experience linear time.

The best way to comprehend this concept is to explore your dreams. In your dreams there is no time lapse between your thoughts and their consequential manifestation, whereas in physical reality energy is slowed down, so it takes time for ideas to physically manifest. Our culture places too much emphasis on the intellect and not enough on intuition. The ego and intellect are necessary in physical reality, but a practical balance with intuition would be beneficial. True solutions and insights spring from our inner selves through our intuition. Like intuition, dreams convey clairvoyant messages regarding opportunities or disasters.

Most people think of the dream state as being unreal and illusionary, when it may be more accurate to say that we go to sleep to experience the real reality and wake to an illusion. Regardless, day-to-day living in the physical world is a very important aspect and adventure for both the physically actualized being, as well as the entire entity. In fact, in the dream state and various times during waking life, on unconscious levels, each earthly person shares lessons and experiences with all other reincarnated selves. Contemplating that concept, you will see that even the most advanced human-developed communication systems are still very elementary and primitive compared to the nature of *ALL THAT IS (God)* and all of it's natural creations.

However, our technologies are merely inventions that come from imaginations of our internal lives. Inventors, poets, artists, writers, architects and every successful person receives his or her ideas and inspirations from dreams and intuition. So the entity will develop a human personality, and this independent identity will select parents from an array of potential parents who may be able to best provide the genetic structure and the lifestyle opportunities that will meet a soul's purposes.

Since consciousness forms matter — contrary to scientific belief — the psychic, psychological and spiritual consciousness creates the biological structure. All chromosomal tissue consists of living data encoded in the DNA itself that is programmed by the inner self. Essentially, as many spirit teachers claim, *your physical bodies are merely spirit-made flesh.* So, as I say many times in my book, **BELIEFOLOGY**, everything is determined by it's consciousness and in order to change your life, it is necessary to transform your consciousness. So it is consciousness that makes the world go round.

The following is a quote from one of my spirit teachers: *"Identity, consciousness acting upon itself knowingly and lovingly, is so rich and varied that no rigid definitions can confine and limit the breadth and expanse of creativity which spills across all realities. Yet, within this vastness of Being, the singularity of each identity's experience of itself is no illusion, but attests to the integrity, dignity, and inviolate nature of all consciousness. Consciousness is an attribute, a divine gift and tool by which each expression of itself explores, defines, and enlarges upon itself, in a myriad unfolding and celebrating,*

Internal Life 175

knowledgefully reveling, protecting, and loving each and every formation springing forth out of the conscious reasoning mind of ALL THAT IS."

So the basic theme to this book, **INTERNAL LIFE**, is that all external experiences, places and things are reflections of inner reality. As the teaching, creating and healing entities proclaim, *"You create your reality."*

Initially, on an ego level, I resisted the idea of possibly losing my personal identity upon death as my consciousness returns to it's over-soul. But if my intuition, perception and interpretations of my spirit teachers' explanations are true, then no identity is ever lost.

All consciousness is always in a state of changing, transforming itself with infinite divine freedom, and expressing it's inexhaustible creative love. If you consider simultaneous time, you will understand how through hypnotism or dreams you can actually revisit your birthday party when you were five years old. And at the same time you are not only the five-year old, but you are your ten, twenty, fifty and sixty-year old self also. Stretch your imagination even further with the concept that all events and experiences are probable. This is paradoxical because, if you accept the concept of simultaneous time, logic would dictate you believe in fate or predestination. However, as we learn more about quantum physics, you are going to hear more and more about parallel universes.

In other words, there is no destiny that can't be changed. We live in a probable system where you are always free to choose and there are probable relationships, jobs and events that aren't physically actualized in your conscious reality, however they are actualized in another parallel universe. In fact, there are an infinite number of physical and non-physical realities. As a spirit teacher once said, *"ALL THAT IS isn't sure whether or not it is the only ALL THAT IS."* This concept only hints at the magnitude and power of *God*.

After the child is born — and sometimes before — the new earthling will start casting others to be in his or her life time drama. Your world has a non-physical origin. The energy/power and mental psyche first has an internal sphere I call *the cosmic casting studio* where all existence has it's inner dimensions. Your personal desires, intent and purpose in your waking reality, in tandem with mutually agreed upon objectives between your soul self, will provide direction for your casting operations in this internal framework environment. The human personality will only manifest those experiences that he or she believes or knows are possible and worthy. *ALL THAT IS (God)*, the universe, or whatever you want to label it, always has a beneficial intent. The universe always desires the best outcome and a beneficial fulfillment for all of it's creations. It is humans, through erroneous beliefs, that acquiesce and attract unfavorable or destructive events.

Events are psychic thought particles that are faster than light. These psychological experiences consist of electromagnetic energy. Let's use the Beatles for illustrative purposes. Each Beatle probably met in this internal casting studio during their infancy (or maybe before birth) to determine what lessons were needed to create Beatlemania. Now, since all events are probable, there were other probable Beatles that could have been manifested instead of Ringo, George, Paul and John. Similarly, there are other children, spouses, friends or relationships that were considered in this inner studio that were never physically actualized. Every relationship and event first takes place in

Internal Life

this inner environment where cooperation and free choice is involved. All thoughts and ideas are charged with electro-magnetic energy that act as magnets that attract to each person certain beliefs and expectations from this inner casting studio into their day-to-day lives. Although there are countless probabilities in this internal framework, only those opportunities that are comparable with the beliefs, expectations and emotions among all involved in any one event in the physical world are manifested.

This explains one of the most essential and important of all of the natural universal laws — *like consciousness attracts like consciousness.* With this in mind, you can see there can be no victims, accidents or coincidences. As a simple example, the robber, the person being robbed and the policeman must share common beliefs in order to attract each other and create the outcome of the robbery.

Likewise, the wealthy person who has the reputation of whatever he or she touches turns to gold, attracts opulent opportunities. Similarly, those people who believe that they are capable and worthy of attracting positive, harmonious and fulfilling relationships will indeed do so. In *BELIEFOLOGY*, I focus on the law of attraction and how you can put it to work in practical ways to transform your consciousness by changing your beliefs. In this book, I focused more on getting in touch with your inner self and your spirit guides, as they can help you navigate along your exciting journey.

Everything has it's source and origin in internal life. Life is merely a smorgasbord of choice and it is important to be inner-directed. Nothing outside ourselves can make us happy, sad, depressed, angry or fulfilled; not even material things, such as a new car or a gorgeous home, for it is the inner feeling or gratification that makes the physical object desirable. No event, experience, place or thing can upset us unless we give *power* to these things outside ourselves. The same is true for outer validation. We are educated, indoctrinated, and conditioned — like Pavloveon dogs — by rewards or punishment instead of learning how to be self-directed, self-fulfilled and self-actualized. It is amazing to me that we, as a collective society, can not understand why there are so many people lacking self-esteem reaching out to the psychological profession and other gurus for solutions and happiness. No one can help, heal or gratify another or make someone else happy. Mental or physical health, joy, fulfillment and pleasure are all inner/internal in nature. Feel more and think less because you heal from the heart and not from your head. There is no one more or less powerful than yourself. No one is more, better, less or worse than anyone else. We are all cherished, loved, divine expressions of *ALL THAT IS.* Your intuition is your direct hot line to your inner selves, as well as to *God.* Listen to this wisdom, and more importantly, act on it's guidance.

All of *God's* creations were spawned from love. You are enough just as you are. Accept yourself for the miraculous, loving, beautiful, creative and powerful person that you are. Listen to the voice of your inner wisdom and allow it to guide you in your preference of choices. If you make choices that bring you undesirable results, then again listen to your "God-self" and know that you are always safe and provided for. Realize that you are deserving of only the very best because you are a living partner with mother-father *God*, not a sinful creature apart and outside of Godhood.

Try not to push events and struggle, but be gentle and accept yourself right now the way you are and allow the magic and the fruitful bounty of life to find you.

CHAPTER 12
FICTIONAL SHORT STORY: Or Is It?

It's a beautiful spring day in 2075 and Freedom and Joy, who are brother and sister, are working on their school assignments. Approximately 40% of all children get home instruction, while the other 60% attend private schools. Lessons are experientially based and self-directed, giving the children the autonomy to explore their own interests. Education has evolved into curriculums that are enjoyable, creative, purposeful, individualized and highly functional and relevant to the times.

Humanity has transformed itself. Each individual is extremely conscious of how he or she creates his or her reality. Collectively, society has made the greatest discovery of all time — the discovery of internal life and how everything springs up from a rich and abundant inner reality.

Shortly after the year 2000, the *outer*-space program evolved into an *inner*-space program when scientists finally began to explore the incredible power and energy within each person. With these adventures, humans began to realize that each and every person is inherently good, powerful, psychic, whole, telepathic and enough, no matter what they have or don't have. They are all gods and goddesses, deserving and worthy of the best!

The authoritarian, paternal institutions of the past all crumbled when people learned they no longer desired to be controlled and assumed total responsibility for their own creations. No longer fragmented, separated, and dissected or compartmentalized, science, medicine and religion merged as leaders in these areas accepted that the mind, body and spirit are essentially all one. Traditional, organized religion ran out of sheep when society finally understood that there is no heaven, hell or devil, and that the only evil is man-made and stemmed from ignorance and powerlessness. Churches were replaced with centers where people now gather for fellowship, and to celebrate and enjoy life!

Technology includes new *in*-ventions such as electromagnetic light and sound that allows buildings to be built and destroyed in mere minutes. Not only did the new understanding of the atom and the *in*-volution of the power of the mind bring innovative tools, but it gave people the capacity to utilize their inner light in order to appear and disappear, just like they did in the old Star Trek program when Captain Kirk ordered: *"Beam me up, Scottie."*

Much like Jesus and other great teachers, the new inner-directed, highly aware and conscious person no longer dies and leaves his or her body. People can now consciously incarnate without leaving remains. Because of DNA programming and the advanced cellular consciousness of humans, only persons born after 2050 can effectively disappear or reappear. Nevertheless, most people realize that all time, including lifetimes, are simultaneous and many use this phenomenon to explore past and future lives. The average life span in 2075 is 200 years, without the physical body deterioration of past generations.

Fictional Short Story

Few laws are necessary because people are personally responsible, self-directed, and realize that to limit, injure, or steal from another will only create a comparable repercussion to self. Reward and punishment systems of earlier centuries are reviewed in school and demonstrated in museum holograms, and people are amazed that past civilizations were so ignorant and limiting. Each person is aware of the multidimensional nature of existence. They have access to all of their life times because, after all, they are happening simultaneously. Furthermore, with the acceptance of simultaneous time, people now embrace their other reincarnational selves and realize that their consciousness is a culmination of all of their life times. With the ability to search past life times, people came to realize that the ignorance of racial and gender prejudice, as well as discrimination were very naïve, since the entirety of their being is comprised of so many different races and genders, both male and female.

Much emphasis is placed on psychic and telepathic training and self-exploration. Children are educated to tap the unlimited reservoirs of their inner skills and energy. History lessons often include time travel where those older earth beings that are unable to disappear and reappear learn to go into a trance and direct themselves to other times. Of course, the younger humans with altered DNA that never limited their cellular consciousness, simply transform physically, returning to other time zones and other previously unknown realities.

For students of all ages, adventures in consciousness and the exploration of self, including the enjoyment and expression of self, is the most important of all lessons. Which brings us back to Joy and her brother, Freedom, who are about to embark on a soul-coasting journey of time traveling genealogy. Their assignment is to discover and review a life when they were together. Previous generations would have referred to this as *past lives*, but Freedom and Joy realize that all of their lives are occurring at once, but at different frequencies. They know that in order to live this lifetime on earth, their atoms and electromagnetic consciousness units must be slowed down so that they can operate physically here on this plane.

Joy and Freedom have the ability to dematerialize and show up in other time zones and other dimensions. However, they are invisible to those people living in these other frequencies. Their genealogy soul-coasting takes them to the physical dimension in the year 2045, at Woodland Cemetery in Dayton, Ohio. Joy and Freedom materialize themselves and are standing in front of a holograve. During the thirties and forties, tombstones were replaced with holograves. Whenever someone approaches the grave, electronic sensors activate a hologram of the departed that appears and presents in their own voice, a brief bio as well as a summary of what life meant to them. Joy and Freedom enjoy a journey through this ancient cemetery, reveling in the history of the likes of the Wright Brothers, who invented the old airplane; Charles Kettering, who had something to do with automobiles; and Paul Lawrence Dunbar, who was a poet. Cemeteries were always fascinating to these two long-distance travelers, since their generation would not need graves. They will simply disappear when they choose to exit their life play.

As they explore the holograves, Freedom discovers that he was Leslie Stewart (a female) in this lifetime and Joy was Kenneth Routson (a male). Leslie died in 2043 and Ken died in 2032. Now Freedom and Joy are extremely excited and become even more inquisitive about their "past reincarnational selves". They set forth to observe these lives. As they concentrate to go back several decades, each of their over-soul guides/teachers appear and explain that it isn't the proper time to witness the actual lives of Ken and Leslie. The children are curious and ask why and the reason is revealed.

Our overall entity is composed of all of our reincarnational selves (past and present), as well as all of our probable selves. Since time/life times are simultaneous/multidimensional certain lessons being experienced by Ken and Leslie will be relevant to the lives of Freedom and Joy. The two clearly understood the multi-dimensionality of life and accepted that Ken and Leslie's lives were still occurring in a simultaneous time. In other words, Freedom and Joy's choices were affecting Ken and Leslie's, and visa versa. At a later date, these guides of their higher selves would escort Joy and Freedom through the excerpts of Ken's and Leslie's lives that were impacting theirs. But in order not to interfere with Freedom and Joy's immediate lessons and personal growth, it was imperative that they not be intimately involved at this time with this "past life".

The teachers from their higher selves agreed to provide them with the physically actualized collective events that transpired from the beginning of the new millennium through Ken's and Leslie's lifetime. The teachers explained that this was the most influential time period in the history of the human race. The following collective events were co-created on earth from 1999 to 2043:

In the year ...	*As more and more people acknowledge the mind-body connection and accept that illness results from an imbalance of one's psychic energy, they leave behind*
1999	*traditional medicine in favor of alternative methods of healing. Doctors must consider new paradigms of preventive medicine and begin to use eclectic holistic approaches instead of the historical practice of treating*

symptoms.

Social Security is privatized.

The United States Constitution is amended to eliminate discrimination because of sexual preferences.

Same sex marriages are legalized.

2000 *Although many holistic practitioners, psychics healers and psychologists are beginning to understand that disease is the result of misdirected energy, unbalanced lifestyle, emotional confusion and erroneous beliefs, a small percentage are now also recognizing the link between inner- and outer-worlds. They understand that true healing comes about by altering/transforming the state of consciousness.*

All ATM/debit cards/machines are replaced by either eye-gaze or fingerprint processes and more purchases are transacted via ATM's, including vending machine services.

Mass marketing of new television technology makes interactive television (where the computer is integrated within the television) more popular. More business, including banking is done via Internet.

There is more and more controversy over schools that teach metaphysics and other "you create your own reality" themes.

2001 *A national sales tax replaces the IRS. The former IRS is reorganized in order to coordinate the collection of this new fair-tax system.*

Female college students proclaim that it is sexist for men to be able to go topless, but not women, and stage topless protests.

Schools, churches and parents begin to understand that happiness is a choice and that drugs and violence are actually caused by lack of self-esteem and a feeling of basic powerlessness. New classes are developed that include discussions on how to be peaceful, joyful, fulfilled and balanced.

2002 Due to lack of resources and in order to promote choice and "real" quality assurance, most public schools begin to be converted to private schools through the voucher system.

Government admits failure of the war on drugs and replaces "war" with programs that promote empowerment, interdependence, self-love and healthy self-esteem.

Less expensive advanced communication technology empowers women in the third world countries to emancipate and demand their equal rights.

2003 State and local governments are encouraged to let go of the past. They remove war relics: cannons, statues featuring men with weapons, etc. Instead of celebrating Memorial Day to focus on wars of the past, there is to be more emphasis on celebrating freedom and life.

The collective awakening creates a new trend where individuals begin to depend less on outer authority and more on trusting inner self, instinct and intuitive senses.

More people take ownership and total responsibility for their feelings, actions and experiences. Fewer people believe or accept victimhood.

Global economy dictates the need for a universal currency.

2004 Much down sizing and reorganizing takes place in national, state and local governments. Legislative representatives are no longer needed since each citizen can now vote on issues direct via the Internet and *interactive television. This reduces the need for campaign financing, and makes the system much more democratic by empowering citizens to represent themselves.*

The citizens of England demand an end to Royalty and urge them to sell off property and donate the proceeds to charities.

Drugs are de-criminalized.

The citizens of the United States elect their first woman president.

2005 *Movie theaters and televisions begin to be replaced by holograms.*

Due to a lack of memberships, many churches shut down. Those that survive become more spiritual and less religious, celebrating life and eliminating control and guilt. These churches believe in a more loving, powerful and androgynous father-mother god. They no longer pay homage to an authoritarian, paternal God.

2006 *Quantum physics scientists collaborate with medical practitioners and mechanical, electronic and nuclear engineers to in-vent prototypes of technology that will utilize light and sound. Much of this technology is possible due to important breakthroughs in the understanding of the nature of the atom and new insights about the nature of consciousness and the universe in general.*

Women's Rights legislation passes, permitting women to go topless in public when desired.

2007 *Other countries follow the example set by the United States, replacing most of the strata of government and its bureaucracy with a collective input via electronic and computer communications. Remaining executive* *representatives of government place the issues up for vote before the general populace. Essentially, each person will act as his or her own representative replacing the cumbersome representation system.*

2008 *The United Nations becomes central headquarters for a type of world government. Not a controlling form of government that previous types of government practiced, but an international center that includes conflict resolution and international trade and business associations (a sort of international chamber of commerce), as well as continuing to serve the traditional roles of the United Nations.*

Local, county, state and federal governments privatize most of their services, including the United States Post Office. In addition, there are efforts to privatize highways, making them all toll roads.

2009 *Parents are concerned because their teen-age children have become fanatical about spending time in trance and altered states. Many teens have time traveled to visit their past and future lives.*

Alternative energy sources, such as lightning and solar power, are utilized. The advent of sound and light technology has developed amazing possibilities and is ready to be marketed and used.

2010 *College students protest in the nude proclaiming there is nothing to be ashamed of, that the human body is beautiful.*

The quantum awakening is even more profound in the collective shift from fear-centered living to love-centered living.

2012 *It is reported throughout the world that children under the age of 13 have been observed levitating objects.*

Legislation passes allowing public nudity.

The acceleration of energy will culminate as the planet and its occupants move into the 5th dimension. This 5th dimensional energy will increase vibration frequencies that will further raise humankind's consciousness and will forever change time and perception and enhance human beings' capabilities. Various characteristics (previously unused) in the DNA will be activated, as well as other transformations in genetic and cellular structures. This increased electric energy will heighten cosmic awareness to the delivery of the new physical planet. Mother Earth, with all of its human, animal and plant species will have finally been reborn with a new consciousness. <u>*There were more transformational changes during this year than any other calendar year in the history of the universe.*</u>

2014 *All people will combine conscious intent with following their impulses and will live more spontaneously and instinctually. Higher levels of conscious awareness result and people realize that they are a vital part of Godhood —any separation is merely an illusion — and power, health, prosperity, joy, peace and fulfillment are the natural birthrights of every human being.*

The first mass-marketed flying automobile (Flymobile) is introduced.

2016 *Any remaining paternal, hierarchical, authoritarian systems begin to crumble when citizens reclaim their power and take personal responsibility for their conscious life creations. Furthermore, such collective empowerment aids the realization that there are no victims and that reward/punishment, as well as judgment concepts and practices are limiting and detrimental. This major paradigm shift and simultaneous global consciousness transformation* decreases the need for most insurance policies, police/fire departments, security systems and regulatory systems and brings about a significant reduction in older traditional medical practices.

2018 Most governments are replaced by self-government and community associations on state and local levels. Globally, there will be continued unification where no one country will be more dominant than another and international committees will govern. Limited tribal turfdom mentality is replaced with the global realization that the only race is the human race. The majority of nations gradually down side their military and enter into an international peace-keeping cooperative.

2020 Although it is challenging for the older generation, the majority of people are taking 100% responsibility in consciously creating their own realities. Science, spiritual groups (formerly religions), health practitioners, educators, business and engineers merge holistically into a new synergy that will totally replace old paradigms and institutions. The world will never be the same, as people discover how everyone and everything is interconnected through consciousness and purpose. This new awareness will culminate in the ultimate mission — to explore, experience and enjoy other dimensions, and the internal life in all things. Finally, humankind will understand that consciousness is the root and cause of everyone and everything and that fulfillment is the intrinsic motivation.

2022 The conscious advancements in the collectively evolved psyche, in tandem with the quantum awakening of cellular and DNA consciousness, has resulted in a heightened interest in developing psychic abilities. People now realize that they are their own power source and make practical use of the energy of

	thought. Unbelievable progress is made in telepathy, mentally moving objects at-will, and consciously attracting chosen things and events into one's life. Channeling becomes as common and popular as the Internet in the last century.
2025	Those beings referred to as extraterrestrial formally introduce themselves. Although they have been earthbound for many years, they decided to reveal themselves once humankind advanced spiritually.
2030	Entities in channeling sessions, along with visions and prophecies from humans, proclaim the coming of a new generation that will have the biological and metaphysical capabilities to physically disappear and reappear.
2032	Ken consciously chooses to permanently exit his body on May 31.
2035	In this century, there has been a proliferation of communication and informational advanced technology. However, the most significant transformation is in human consciousness. Although many older people are dependent on the near obsolete Internet-hologram, the younger generation is stimulated by the inner-net experience. Via conscious dream state or trance, they can explore not only past, present, and future events, but they can also journey to cosmic libraries, as well as other dimensions and realities.
2040	New extraterrestrial are popping in from all over the universe, offering earth beings many new ideas and technologies.
2043	Leslie consciously decides to leave her body on November 27, so that she may prepare for another life with Ken in 2059.

Fictional Short Story

Young Freedom and Joy were amazed at the things Ken and Leslie had experienced in their life time: from the evolution of black and white television to the ability of humans to manipulate matter through their thoughts and emotions. Clearly technology progressed much quicker than the social and spiritual evolution. It wasn't until the end of this past life for Joy and Freedom, that true natural spirituality became a reality.

Joy and Freedom were elated with their adventure and shared the things they learned on their journey with their friends. This assignment finished, they encouraged others to soul-coast as they jumped back into the inner-net to get a glimpse of some of their *future* selves.

Is this short story reality or fiction? You must decide for yourself. . .

Explore your internal reality through all of your past, present and future selves by consciously entering your dreams. Examining your dreams can reveal the nature and causes of your *external* life. Take some time to write in your journal. As you document your dreams and the details of what appear to be simply coincidences, you will begin to see a pattern of synchronicities between your experiences throughout your life's journey.

May your spirit soar with the strength of an eagle and the beauty of a butterfly. May you radiate with every fiber of your being the eternal, unconditional love and joy that is your natural inheritance. May this enlightenment be a beacon to help others ignite their passionate spirit. Realize that by being and believing in your *self*, you germinate the powerful seeds of infinite possibilities. Being and expressing unconditional love and joy fulfills not only your individual purpose but that of the universal eternal *Internal Life!*

APPENDIX ❖ ❖ ❖ ❖ ❖ ❖ ❖

The following are the author's responses to typical questions asked at his metaphysical seminars.

1. **What is the purpose of dreams?**
    It is my perception that multidimensional dream realities are the coordinators and facilitators of the living psyche. Dreams have at least two major functions. First, dream cycles provoke chemical reactions that affect hormonal and other glandular and metabolic processes. Without dreams, the physical body could not exist nor would there be any psychic activity because dreams rejuvenate mind, body and spirit. Second, dreams assist intuition in keeping the physical self in touch with all of the inner selves. They are sort of like the cosmic super glue that gives an entity a sense of identity. Besides providing the physical self with messages from the inner self that are intense enough to get through to ego self, the dream forum collaborates between the inner selves and the physical probable selves with planning, directing, and manifesting physical events and experiences.
    According to *Seth*, even plants, trees, animals and insects dream as they translate their internal lives into physical lives.
    The more I explore my dreams, the more I can enter the dream state consciously and become a conscious co-creator in my dreams. Often in this reality and sometimes in other realities in her dreams, Leslie (my partner), remembers assisting others in their healings. I highly recommend that you to explore the various unknown realities in your dreams as well as become aware of your internal life in the dream state!

2. **Do you believe in Karma?**
    Some people think of karma as a sort of punishment from God for something they have done in a past life. I do not subscribe to this definition because I don't believe in a judgmental God that is into punishment or any other recriminations. Others believe karma is a predestined fate. This, too, I discount because I believe that we can always choose to change our probabilities and that at any moment you can alter your past or future. Nevertheless, I do believe in the power of attraction; therefore, I think karma is the vibration or the force generated by each person's consciousness.
    I once heard it expressed that karma is simply unfinished action. Now, I am not saying that someone cannot have a belief in

karma as punishment and not attract negative consequences. After all, we do create our realities in accordance with our beliefs, emotions and expectations. However, there is no force outside of us that deals with rewards or punishments. *WE* create our reality.

3. *Is the ego bad?*

It is fascinating that in our society psychologists, counselors and self-empowerment leaders often place much emphasis on eliminating, reducing or at least taming the ego. First, it is important to realize that without the ego the personality could *NOT* exist in the physical environment. The inner self cannot function in a linear time structure; therefore, the ego is necessary for general direction of the physical personality.

As you can detect in your dreams, there is no ego, and thus, no structural organization. Now the aforementioned professionals are correct in the assumption that when the EGO is out of balance, there are detrimental consequences. The ego is a natural needed component of the whole self. However, when the ego becomes rigid, or feels too important it restricts the flow of expression and impulses from the inner selves and the basic needs of the *whole* self are limited. When this happens, either mental or physical illness will manifest, or even suicidal tendencies will show up.

Much of the spiritual evolution that is taking place in our world is based on the the recognition that historically, we developed basically either a male or female personality, both as individuals and as organizations and institutions. But we are beginning to understand that we are not only more than the physical, but there are many other life expressions occurring simultaneously. Furthermore, we are discovering that much of our social problems are the result of institutions and dogma that has its framework immersed in an ego-bound, male authoritarian consciousness. Our individual epiphanies and awakenings will guide us to integrate the masculine and the feminine, the intuitive and the intellect, and the inner psyche with the ego.

The mass collective consciousness of society will then reflect this healthy balance of the ego and inner self and will produce future communities based on unconditional love, acceptance, health, personal responsibility, prosperity, and harmonious relationships.

4. *Do you believe in the Devil?*

I believe any devil is a hallucination of anyone alive or dead that believes there is such a creature. Those persons who believe in hell and the devil may, out of fear, create such a drama upon death or possibly before in the dream state. Therefore, just as we create our reality by our feelings and beliefs while we are in physical form, we do the same in the after-life.

Like earth life, all events are temporary, and after death, if you do believe in hell and the devil, through role-playing your guides and teachers will assist you to move away from such restrictive, limiting and fearful dramas.

As far as evil, I believe that any thing that is limiting, fearful or anti-life is the only evil that exists. As I say in *BELIEFOLOGY*, "evil" is "live" spelled backwards. No thing, nothing, has power over us at any time, either in or out of physical existence *unless* we give it the power over us! Life and the universe are always for us and we are meant to be life-affirming beings — not fearful and restricted victims.

5. ***Why does it seem that so many people who are in metaphysics have problems with manifesting prosperity or harmonious relationships?***

I think that people who are into subjects such as metaphysics and the *SETH MATERIAL* are basically pretty mental and rely much on their intellect. I know this from personal experience and through working with students that we mental people have a tendency to analyze things to the last gnat's eyebrow. I have discovered that allowing abundance, whether it is attracting money, relationships, jobs or opportunities requires trust and feeling. Remember that it takes *e*-motion in order to elctromagnetically fuel ideas and expectations. The way people who come from an intellectual framework often con themselves when doing belief work is by using rationalizations or denials instead of taking ownership of all of their beliefs and feelings. Although there is the need for the intellect, we often underestimate the benefits of the intuition.

On the other hand, there are those people who may be more emotional without a healthy balance with the intellect and I have found some of these individuals are gullible. They may subscribe to any belief, guru or organization without healthy skepticism.

Finally, I think the major impediments to allowing the flow of prosperity in are in the areas of deservability, worthiness, trust and the belief of scarcity. Although you may think you have eliminated erroneous beliefs regarding the aforementioned, at times there are some beliefs remaining that the universe is not safe and we cannot trust in ourselves or others because of "man's" very nature. Moreover, when we believe that we are born with sin although we do all the "right" affirmations and visualizations, we never seem to feel that we are enough. In addition, I have met many people in the so-called *New Age* movement who came from previous involvement in eastern religions with beliefs such as desire is bad, celibacy is healthy and attempts to become selfless and reach nirvana are good.

In other words, sometimes what we *think* we believe in isn't what we really believe. Observe your feelings, reactions and responses to events, as well as your day-to-day reality and then you will see what you truly believe.

6. ***Explain Simultaneous Time.***
Our physical world is a three-dimensional materialization of our mental and psychic environments. Our physical and planetary universe is simultaneous existing at once in time and space. Consciousness always creates form and each emotion and thought has its own electromagnetic energy that slows down and translates into physical reality. I think that one of the major purposes of physical reality is to provide us with a forum to see how our thoughts, beliefs, emotions and expectations create our day-to-day existence. Our next frontier is to become conscious co-creators and to learn how to consciously create our reality of choice.

The following are two examples I often use to explain simultaneous time. When you watch television, can your physical television tune into all of the channels at once? If it could, would you be able to comprehend all of the programming at once? All of the programs, soap operas and sports events have already be produced (except for the live shows), but because of three-dimensional reality, you can only choose to focus on limited amounts of activity. Likewise, your con-current reincarnational life times are occurring simultaneously, but you have your focus on this one. In other words, in this life time, you are simultaneously that child at your fifth birthday and the eighty-year old deciding to exit this life's expression.

What appears contradictory and extremely paradoxical is that, although this appears to be evidence of fate, this too is an illusion because within simultaneous time is the theory that everything is probable (See the following on probabilities).

7. ***Seth talks about probable selves, multidimensional selves, and the probable system. Can you elaborate?***
You are a part of a spontaneous cosmic play where you have many various selves expressing themselves in many diverse ways. Every

actor has full freedom to author each play and to respond to any event created.

Although you have other parts of your overall entity creating dramas in other life times, each personality retains its own identity. During the dream state, between lives, and even while you are awake, on unconscious levels each multidimensional self is aware of each of the other selves. Our culture perceives things that are physical as real and valid, and any phenomenon that you can't see, touch, hear or feel as non-real and invalid. In actuality, the soul is a culmination of infinite creative acts that express themselves in unlimited dimensions in order to fulfill infinite possibilities. Your life (even day-to-day, moment-to-moment) is the result of an endless *choice* of actions. All of your day dreams and creative imaginings according to *Seth* are manifested in some probable reality. Perhaps some of these realities are physical, while others are in dream-like realities. The *Sethian* assumption is that **ALL** probable realities are just as real, valid and fulfilled, even if they are non-physical.

As author, director, choreographer and actor of your life creations, you constantly select each event/experience in your plan. Anyone agreeing to be a part of your drama will collaborate in planning the "next" event, either consciously in this reality or in what *Seth* refers to as *Framework II*. Now, out of many probable possibilities, every character in any event will physically actualize those experiences that each actor believes, knows or expects as possible. For all the characters, opportunities or events that are not physically actualized will manifest in another reality, thus benefiting and fulfilling the overall soul. Consider this analogy: Remember the cliffhanger season finale of *Dallas*, when the producer had actors and actresses tape several versions of different people shooting J.R., and only a few individuals knew which "probability" would be played on national television. In our physical day-to-day living, we too have various scenarios and will only physically actualize those experiences that are in correlation with our beliefs and it is usually those mental dramas that have the greatest emotional intensities.

8. ***Can you talk a little about Earth changes?***
First, it is important to remember that earth is very similar to our biology because it is a conscious, living, breathing, always changing organism. Earth is not of the same level of consciousness as humans, but nevertheless, it consists of awarized energy that is interwoven with all of creaturehood, including the human species. Our spiritual

consciousness will determine how our DNA, endocrine systems, and all other biological functions develop and operate, as well as how they interact with the earth and creaturehood therein. Furthermore, in tandem with this process is cosmic energy including the sun, gamma rays, asteroids and comets that affect light/sound filaments of creaturehood and the rest of earth matter.

The oversouls who co-created our solar system have joined forces with our oversouls and any inner selves/entities that plan to enter our reality. The collective agenda is to awaken the consciousness of human kind and assist them in reaching a much higher level of awareness and consciousness. A large part of this plan is to accelerate the energy and increase the vibrations. This will afford the earth and its inhabitants the opportunity to *gradually* move from a third dimension into a fourth and finally a fifth dimension. Consequently, this will result in significant changes in the spiritual, psychic, physical, cellular and electromagnetic consciousness. Consciousness forms matter, therefore, dynamic shifts will *gradually* occur within the geological, magnetic, and the meteorological functions of our earth. As we humans increase our vibration, we will affect the magnetic field that we share with the earth and the earthly magnetic grids will adjust.

As I say in my book, *BELIEFOLOGY*, mother earth and all of its inhabitants are in labor, bringing forth a birth of a new mass consciousness. The spiritual revolution that is happening on inner levels will transform economics, politics, the environment, education and medicine, and thus create a social/planetary evolution. All of this will culminate in earth healing itself and other unbelievable earth changes. From 1995 to 2015, we will continue to see drastic changes in weather patterns including more severe tornadoes, hurricanes, droughts, and floods than we have ever seen since humans have recorded meteorological and geological events. Yes, beliefs create emotion and *e*-motion propels ideas to reality. In addition, the chemicals from *e*-motion co-create the weather. When you combine many people with emotional storms, you create weather storms.

Those persons who are caught in the middle of some of these growing pangs may perceive it as a negative thing. However, in the greater scheme of the universe, these changes are not only beneficial, but necessary in order for humans to continue on the earth plane.

There will be many people who will choose to not make this significant transformation in consciousness. Some will be killed in natural disasters, while others will die from various illnesses. Follow your inner guidance and then you will always be in the right place, successfully engaged in the right activity. Your inner selves and guides will inform you of possible danger and you can move either temporarily or permanently to safer environments.

Always remember that you create your reality and that you can create a safe universe for yourself, no matter what may be happening around you!

9. ***What is your view on abortion?***
No one can kill or eradicate a soul!! There are no victims and the souls who choose those mothers who may choose to end the pregnancy know the probabilities. Nevertheless, I believe it is more beneficial for both males and females to be proactive and responsible in order to prevent the need for abortion in the first place. Unfortunately, I do think some of the souls seeking entry into this physical reality are emotionally hurt when they are aborted. I do believe that in many cases, the abortion occurs when a pregnancy is simply biological because of non-committed or uncertain souls who aren't sure if they want the earthly challenges. Maybe the many miscarriages and sudden infant death occurrences are also children who may have changed their minds.

Abortion can create much guilt and stress for some potential mothers. I know one woman who attended one of my classes said that she has spent ten years running from one psychologist to another unable to shake her guilt. She even attracted ovarian cancer to punish herself for her self-inflicted guilt. She later told me that after that one class where I shared my view on abortion, she was finally able to release all of her guilt and self-punishments.

10. ***What do you mean when you say you are not religious, but spiritual?***
My definition of religion is scrupulous conformity to institutionalized, authoritative dogmatic tenets. In most religions, you are requested not to question their dogma, but to just have faith and **obey** God's will. Often, most religions either believe or talk as if their God is a paternal, judgmental authority who is separate from "his" creations. Many religions believe that God will reward those who are baptized with eternal heaven, as well as those who worship, obey and are either good or show remorse and plead/pray for forgiveness. Much of religion's focus is on suffering and sacrifice. The *Bible* is the foundation for many religions and the *Old Testament* is based on fear. Jesus came to enlighten the world with his message of trust, faith and unconditional love. I believe one of Jesus' major missions was to

encourage people to take away the control from religions and to gain their freedom by developing a spiritual relationship with God and their neighbors, based on love. Consequently, the *New Testament* was developed. Unfortunately, even after Christ's influence, the old control/fear framework was so established by religious and governmental bureaucracies, that Christ's message was misinterpreted because of these old mass belief systems.

Now, to me, spirituality is the recognition that we are the spirit and expression of God consciousness, that is borrowing a physical vehicle (bodies) to enjoy and express the journey of heart and mind on the earth plane. Spirituality is the realization of a divine intent that every being becomes self-realized, grandly powerful, immensely fulfilled, joyful, creative, co-creators who are fully engaged with savoring life!

Instead of limiting spirituality to a certain day of the week, we should live our lives knowing we are the Gods and Goddesses that were created from an infinite love for the purposes of endless love, creativity and joyful fulfillment. True spirituality is the awareness that we are not separate from God, but in an internal/eternal partnership and sacred connection with every other universal being and all living forms. It is each individual declaring his/her individual declaration of independence by reclaiming his/her personal power and letting go of attach- ments, fears and doubts, knowing and trusting that life is for us and the best is finding us all.

Furthermore, real spirituality is the unconditional acceptance of all beings, feeling worthy, knowing we all deserve to be here.

Spirituality is always life affirming. Spirituality is about the state of oneness with all life, the tolerance, acceptance and unconditional love of self, others and nature.

11. *In your book, BELIEFOLOGY, you say that judgement is imiting. Can you elaborate?*

First, it is important to discern the difference between a judgement that implies a right/wrong or good and bad versus a judgement that is an evaluation or simply an observation.

Negative judgement is the result of fear and the inability to have confidence in self and the universe. When you judge, you create a bondage between you and what it is you are judging. Thus, we create the blame/shame game. Judgment perpetuates an endless cycle that keeps us stuck to what it is we are blaming. Another by-product of judgement is guilt and guilt seeks out punishment. When we accuse others or ourselves of wrong-doing, we often attract illness, accidents or others that will judge us.

12. **Do you believe in tithing?**
Many religions believe that everyone should donate 10% of their earnings to the church. I have an interesting story about tithing that includes a coincidence I would like to share with you.

One day on my way to my post office box, I was listening to a tape of one of my favorite self-help lecturers, Wayne Dyer. He was talking about tithing, and about how he and others tithe by contributing to whatever source that provides them with spiritual inspiration. This could be an individual, church, author, teacher or organization. I parked my car and entered the post office and guess what was waiting for me in my mail box? Someone who had the same tithing belief as Wayne Dyer mailed me a check accompanied by a touching note that expressed her appreciation for my book, **BELIEFOLOGY**, and how it has been inspirational and beneficial to her life.

ABOUT THE AUTHOR ❖ ❖ ❖ ❖ ❖ ❖ ❖

Ken Routson has been a student and a teacher of metaphysics for over twenty years. He travels throughout the country conducting seminars, workshops and individual classes on *Stress Reduction, Conflict Resolution, Self-Improvement/Empowerment*, the *SETH MATERIAL* and *Beliefology*. Ken's book **BELIEFOLOGY: Raising Your Consciousness to Wealth, Health and Happiness** and the companion workbook, demonstrate how your beliefs and emotions create your reality. In 1984, he formed *Individual Growth and Fulfillment*, a consulting company to help individuals and agencies learn to be empowered and fulfilled.

Ken Routson is nationally recognized for his contributions in the areas of transportation and residential services for individuals who are elderly or disabled. He has served as Executive Director and C.E.O. for organizations that specialize in providing these services and has been a consultant to many corporations, organizations and school districts throughout the United States.

Ken's next project will be to incorporate his management skills with his metaphysical experiences to develop a unique form of life-coaching services. This is just one reason why a prominent social services lecturer/consultant says, *"Ken seems to relish challenges and believes that the future is to be invented, not predicted."*

We hope you enjoyed this Tulip Press book.

If you would like additional copies of **INTERNAL LIFE: I Do Believe in Spirit** or to order any of Ken Routson's other titles, you can place a credit card order by calling: 1-800-388-1945.

Or for shop-by-mail convenience, send a check or money order for $12.95 + $3.00 shipping and handling to:

Tulip Press
P.O. Box 181212
Fairfield, OH 45018

INTERNAL LIFE: I Do Believe In Spirit makes a wonderful gift to give to family and friends. Just let us know who the book is for and we will make sure the book is personalized and autographed by Ken Routson.

Please list the name(s) you would like on the personal message:

_____

_____

_____

For more information regarding services provided by Gordon Stonehouse/*Amel* or Jeff King/*Teach*, you can contact them direct:

Rev. Gordon J. Stonehouse
760-366-0504
63-224 Pole Road
Joshua Tree, CA 92252-4401

Jeff King
c/o Jeffco
P.O. Box 117140
Carrollton, TX 75011-7140
E-mail: JKINGEDU@AOL.com